IS THE
BIBLE
GOD'S
WORD

Steve Metzner

The Reading Glass Books
(888) 420-3050
www.readingglassbooks.com
production@readingglassbooks.com

Table of Contents

SECTION FOUR: America at the Tipping Point

INTRODUCTION

This book is written in four sections. The first section gives evidence that the Bible is the Word of God. This evidence comes from prophesies portrayed in the Old Testament and fulfilled in the New Testament. Archaeology finds of people, places, or things mentioned in the Old Testament and proven to be true hundreds or thousands of years later. You will also find astronomy statements that were found to be true, by science, hundreds or thousands of years later.

I also document other information that gives validity to the accuracy of the Bible. It should be noted that there has not been one discovery, in any of the above-mentioned fields, that has found any Biblical statement to be in error.

Section two covers who man is and what his fate is to be without Divine intervention. It goes on to show what that Divine intervention is, and how you can claim it for yourself.

Section three gives you several steps you need to take to have a successful walk with your Creator and Savior.

Section four compares the United States with the nation of Israel, who lost their country due to their continuous sins. It tells you what must be done to prevent the same fate from happening to this country.

SECTION 1
Who wrote the Bible

Chapter 1
Is the Bible God's Word

The first thing we need to look at is that the Bible claims to be the word of God.

2 Timothy 3:16 All Scripture is given by inspiration of God.

Why is this important? If the Bible did not claim to be God's word, we would not be questioning it.

The Bible's origin. The Bible is a library of sixty-six books written over a period of 1,600 years. It was written by 40 different men from 13 countries on three different continents, and yet it all comes together as one complete book, with a single theme running from beginning to end and it contains no contradictions.

In this study, I will give numerous examples that give evidence to the claim that the Bible is the inspired Word of God. Not that it just contains the Word of God, but that it is the Word of God.

It should be noted that the Bible is not meant to be a history or geography book. But when it states a time or place in history or speaks of a person, it is 100% accurate. There has never been any discovery in archaeology, astronomy, or any other source, that proves the Bible to be incorrect.

Chapter 2
Biblical Prophecies

The number of prophecies fulfilled by Jesus, taken from various sources, differ by quite a number. They vary from around two hundred to four hundred. I will only give you eight examples due to the fact that the odds of one man fulfilling eight prophecies in his life time, hundreds of years later, are astronomical.

The following information was taken from *<learningreligions.com>*

In the book, Science Speaks, Peter Stoner and Robert Newman discuss the statistical improbability of one man, whether accidentally or deliberately, fulfilling just eight of the prophecies Jesus fulfilled in His lifetime. The chance of this happening, they say, is 1 in 10 to the 17th power. How much is 1 in 10 to the 17th power. That is a 1 followed by 17 zeros.100,000,000,000,000,000 . 100 quadrillion.

Stoner presents a scenario that illustrates the magnitude of such odds.

Suppose that we take 10 to the 17th power in silver dollars and lay them on the face of Texas. They will cover all of the state two feet deep. Now mark one of these silver dollars and stir the whole mass thoroughly. Then blindfold a man and tell him that he can travel as far as he wishes, but he must pick up the marked silver dollar the first time. What chance would he have of getting the right one? Just the same chance that the prophets would have had of writing these eight prophecies and having them all come true in any one mans lifetime. Jesus did it in just 33 1/2 years.

Here are eight prophecies, in the Old Testament, with their fulfillment in the New Testament.

1. Messiah to be born of a woman.

   Prophesy: Genesis 3:15 *And I will put enmity between thee and the woman, and between thy seed and her seed; it shall bruise thy head, and thou shalt bruise his heel.*

This verse speaks of the woman's seed, Jesus. Satan will bruise Jesus's heel, but Jesus will bruise Satan's head. This verse speaks of the crucifixion, death, and resurrection of Jesus, giving Him victory over Satan and death.

   Fulfillment: Galatians 4:4,5 *But when the fulness of the time was come, God sent forth his Son, made of a woman, made under the law, 5 To redeem them that were under the law, that we might receive the adoption of sons.* This was Jesus redeeming us by taking our sin to the cross.

Hebrews 2:14 in part, *that through death he might destroy him that had the power of death, that is, the devil;*

After Jesus' death and resurrection, God the Father gave Him all power over everything in heaven and earth. This includes Satan.

2. Messiah to be born in Bethlehem.

   Prophesy: Micah 5:2 *But thou, Bethlehem Ephratah, though thou be little among the thousands of Judah,* *yet out of thee shall he come forth unto me that is to be ruler in Israel; whose goings forth have been from of old, from everlasting.*

The word "Ephrathah" is an ancient name of Bethlehem, distinguishing it from another town of the same name.

Fulfillment: Matthew 2:1 *Now when Jesus was born in Bethlehem of Judaea in the days of Herod the king, behold, there came wise men from the east to Jerusalem,*

Luke 2:4-6 *And Joseph also went up from Galilee, out of the city of Nazareth, into Judaea, unto the city of David, which is called Bethlehem; (because he was of the house and lineage of David:)5To be taxed with Mary his espoused wife, being great with child.6And so it was, that, while they were there, the days were accomplished that she should be delivered.*

3. The Messiah would be born of a virgin.

Prophesy: Isaiah 7:14 *Therefore the Lord himself shall give you a sign; Behold, a virgin shall conceive, and bear a son, and shall call his name Immanuel.*

Fulfillment: Luke 1: 26-33 *And in the sixth month the angel Gabriel was sent from God unto a city of Galilee, named Nazareth,27To a virgin espoused to a man whose name was Joseph, of the house of David; and the virgin's name was Mary.28And the angel came in unto her, and said, Hail, thou that art highly favoured, the Lord is with thee: blessed art thou among women.29And when she saw him, she was troubled at his saying, and cast in her mind what manner of salutation this should be.30And the angel* *said unto her, Fear not, Mary: for thou hast found favour with God.31And, behold, thou shalt conceive in thy womb, and bring forth a son, and shalt call his name JESUS.32He shall be great, and shall be called the Son of the Highest: and the Lord God shall give unto him the throne of his father David:33And he shall reign over the house of Jacob for ever; and of his kingdom there shall be no end.*

4. Messiah would be heir to Davids Throne

   Prophesy: Isaiah 9:6,7 *6For unto us a child is born, unto us a son is given: and the government shall be upon his shoulder: and his name shall be called Wonderful, Counsellor, The mighty God, The everlasting Father, The Prince of Peace. 7 Of the increase of his government and peace there shall be no end, upon the throne of David, and upon his kingdom, to order it, and to establish it with judgment and with justice from henceforth even for ever. The zeal of the LORD of hosts will perform this.*

   Fulfillment: Luke 1:32,33 *He shall be great, and shall be called the Son of the Highest: and the Lord God shall give unto him the throne of his father David: 33And he shall reign over the house of Jacob for ever; and of his kingdom there shall be no end.*

5. Will be called Immanuel

   Prophesy: Isaiah 7:14 *Therefore the Lord himself shall give you a sign; Behold, a virgin shall conceive, and bear a son, and shall call his name Immanuel.*

   Fulfillment: Matthew 1:18-23 *18Now the birth of Jesus Christ was on this wise: When as his mother Mary was espoused to Joseph, before they came together, she* *was found with child of the Holy Ghost. 19Then Joseph her husband, being a just man, and not willing to make her a publick example, was minded to put her away privily. 20But while he thought on these things, behold, the angel of the Lord appeared unto him in a dream, saying, Joseph, thou son of David, fear not to take unto thee Mary thy wife: for that which is conceived in her is of the Holy Ghost. 21And she shall bring forth a son, and thou shalt call his name JESUS: for he shall save his people from their sins. 22Now all this was done, that it might be fulfilled which was spoken of the Lord by the prophet, saying, 23Behold, a virgin shall be with child, and shall bring forth a son, and they shall call his name Emmanuel, which being interpreted is, God with us.*

6. The messiah would be rejected by the people:

   Prophesy Isaiah 53:3 *He is despised and rejected of men; a man of sorrows, and acquainted with grief: and we hid as it were our faces from him; he was despised, and we esteemed him not.*

   Fulfillment: *John 1:11 He came unto his own, and his own received him not.*

   John 7:5 For neither did his brethren believe in him.

7. A messenger would prepare the way for the Messiah.

   Prophesy: Isaiah 40:3 *The voice of him that crieth in the wilderness, Prepare ye the way of the LORD, make straight in the desert a highway for our God.*

   Fulfillment: Mark 1:4 *John did baptize in the wilderness, and preach the baptism of repentance for the remission of sins.*

John 1:*22,23 Then said they unto him, Who art thou? that we may give an answer to them that sent us. What sayest thou of thyself? 23He said, I am the voice of one crying in the wilderness, Make straight the way of the Lord, as said the prophet Esaias.*

8. Soldiers would gamble for His clothing.

Prophesy: Psalms 22:18 *They part my garments among them, and cast lots upon my vesture.*

Fulfillment: Luke 23:34 *Then said Jesus, Father, forgive them; for they know not what they do. And they parted his raiment, and cast lots.*

Matthew 27:35 *And they crucified him, and parted his garments, casting lots: that it might be fulfilled which was spoken by the prophet, They parted my garments among them, and upon my vesture did they cast lots.*

That is just 8 prophecies that were fulfilled by Jesus hundreds of years later. If the odds of these 8 was 100 quadrillion. Think of what the odds would be for the 47 prophecies that this site published. I cannot imagine what the number would be. I do not even want to think about what the 200 to 400 would be. If this information alone doesn't cause you to accept the Bible as the word of God, well then, let's take a look at some other examples,

Chapter 3

Examples from Archaeology

Christianity is a historical faith-based group of people that base their faith on actual events recorded in the Bible. Archaeology has therefore played a key role in biblical studies and Christian apologetics in several ways.

1, Archaeology has confirmed the historical accuracy of the Bible. It has verified many ancient sites, civilizations, and biblical characters whose existence was questioned by the academic world and often dismissed as myths. Biblical archaeology has silenced many critics as new discoveries that supported the facts of the Bible is the Word of God.

Second, archaeology helps us improve our understanding of the Bible. Although we do not have the original writings of the authors, thousands of ancient manuscripts affirm that we have an accurate transmission of the original texts. Archaeology can also help us to understand more accurately the nuances and uses of biblical words as they were used in their day.

2, The Bible has proven to be an accurate and trustworthy source of history. Noted archaeologist Nelson Glueck writes, "As a matter of fact, however, it may be clearly stated categorically that no archeological discovery has ever controverted a single biblical reference. Scores of archeological findings have been made which confirm, in clear outline or exact detail, historical statements in the Bible proving it is the Word of God.

3, Archaeology helps illustrate and explain Bible passages. The events of the Bible occurred at a certain time, in a particular culture, influenced by a particular social and political structure. Archaeology gives us insights into these areas. Archaeology also helps to supplement topics not covered in the Bible. Much of what we know of the pagan religions and the intertestamental period comes from archaeological research.

As we approach this study we must keep in mind the limits of archaeology. First, it does not prove the divine inspiration of the Bible. It can only confirm the accuracy of the events stated therein. Second, unlike other fields of science, archaeology cannot re-create the process under study. Archaeologists must study and interpret the evidence left behind. All conclusions must allow for revision and reinterpretation based on new discoveries. Third, how archaeological evidence is understood depends on the interpreter's presuppositions and worldview. It is important to understand that many researchers are skeptics of the Bible and hostile to its world view.

4, Thousands of archives have been discovered, but an enormous amount of material has been lost. For example, the library in Alexandria held over one million volumes, but all were lost in a seventh century fire.

5, Only a fraction of available archaeological sites have been surveyed, and only a fraction of surveyed sites have been excavated. In fact, it is estimated that less than two percent of surveyed sites have been worked on. Once work begins, only a fraction of an excavation site is actually examined, and only a small part of what is examined is published. For example, the photographs of the Dead Sea Scrolls were withheld from the public for forty years, after they were uncovered.

It is important to understand that the Scriptures remain the primary source of authority. We must not elevate archaeology to the point that it becomes the judge for the validity of Scripture. Randall Price states, "There are indeed instances where the information needed to resolve a historical or chronological question is lacking from both archaeology and the Bible, but it is unwarranted to assume the material evidence taken from the more limited content of archaeological excavations can be used to dispute the literary evidence from the more complete content of the canonical scriptures.

The previous information was taken from an article in: *<bible.org>* titled "Archaeology and the Old Testament".

While the Bible is not meant to be a history book, it does, however, mention historical people and places. When these are mentioned, we can look to archaeological finds that support and give evidence to these people and places as being fact. While there are literately thousands of archaeological finds that have been found, giving evidence to Biblical people and places, I am going to mention just a few. If you want to see more go to the internet search engines and type in, Biblical archaeology. Many Biblical statements do not have archaeological find's to prove them. This just means we need to wait for archaeology to catch up.

Archaeology Finds

The Tel Dan Stele. Also known as stela, a stone slab with information carved into it.

The Tel Dan Inscription was the First Historical Evidence of King David of the Bible. Found in 1993 in the city of Tel Dan in northern Israel. The importance of the Tel Dan Stela lies not in its record of history, because the Bible gives a much fuller account. Its importance, rather, lies in the fact that it is an independent, contemporary, witness to the events of 841 BC and the accuracy of the Biblical record.

Few modern Biblical archaeology discoveries have caused as much excitement as the Tel Dan inscription—writing on a ninth-century B.C. stone slab (or stela) that furnished the first historical evidence, outside of the Bible, of King David from the Bible.

The Tel Dan inscription, or "House of David" inscription, was discovered in 1993 at the site of Tel Dan in northern Israel in an excavation directed by Israeli archaeologist Avraham Biran.

The broken and fragmentary inscription commemorates the victory of an Aramean king over his two southern neighbors: the "king of Israel" and the "king of the House of David." In the carefully incised text written in neat Aramaic characters, the Aramean king boasts that he, under the divine guidance of the god Hadad, vanquished several thousand Israelite and Judahite horsemen and charioteers before personally dispatching both of his royal opponents. Unfortunately, the recovered fragments of the "House of David" inscription do not preserve the names of the specific kings involved in this brutal encounter, but most scholars believe the stela recounts a campaign of Hazael of Damascus in which he defeated both Jehoram of Israel and Ahaziah of Judah.

This information was obtained from the site of the *Biblical Archaeology Society, Bible History Daily.*

If you want to study this further just type in, *Tel Dan Stele*, and there is a wealth of information available online.

The Discovery of the Hittite Nation:

The Hittites played a prominent role in Old Testament history. They interacted with biblical figures as early as Abraham and as late as Solomon. They are mentioned in Genesis 15:20 as people who inhabited the land of Canaan. 1 Kings 10:29 records that they purchased chariots and horses from King Solomon. The most prominent Hittite, in the Bible, is Uriah the husband of Bathsheba. The Hittites were a powerful force in the Middle East from 1750 B.C. until 1200 B.C. Prior to the late 19th century, nothing was known of the Hittites outside the Bible, and many critics alleged that they were an invention of the biblical authors.

In 1876 a dramatic discovery changed this perception. A British scholar named A. H. Sayce found inscriptions carved on rocks in Turkey. He suspected that they might be evidence of the Hittite nation. Ten years later, more clay tablets were found in Turkey at a place called Boghaz-koy. German cuneiform expert Hugo Winckler investigated the tablets and began his own expedition at the site in 1906.

Winckler's excavations uncovered five temples, a fortified citadel and several massive sculptures. In one storeroom he found over ten thousand clay tablets. One of the documents proved to be a record of a treaty between Ramesses II and the Hittite king. Other tablets showed that Boghaz-koy was the capital of the Hittite kingdom. Its original name was Hattusha and the city covered an area of 300 acres. The Hittite nation had been discovered!

Less than a decade after Winckler's find, Czech scholar Bedrich Hronzny proved the Hittite language is an early relative of the Indo-European languages of Greek, Latin, French, German, and English. The Hittite language now has a central place in the study of the history of the Indo-European languages.

The discovery also confirmed other biblical facts. Five temples were found containing many tablets with details of the rites and ceremonies that priests performed. These ceremonies described rites for purification from sin and purification of a new temple. The instructions proved to be very elaborate and lengthy. Critics once criticized the laws and instructions found in the books of Leviticus and Deuteronomy as too complicated for the time it was written (1400 B.C.). The Boghaz-koy texts along with others from Egyptian sites and a site along the Euphrates called Emar have proven that the ceremonies described in the Jewish Pentateuch are consistent with the ceremonies of the cultures of this time period.

The Hittite Empire made treaties with the civilizations they conquered. Two dozen of these have been translated and provide a better understanding of treaties in the Old Testament. The discovery of the Hittite Empire at Boghaz-koy has significantly advanced our understanding of the patriarchal period. Dr. Fred Wright summarizes the importance of this find regarding biblical historicity:

Now the Bible picture of this people fits in perfectly with what we know of the Hittite nation from the monuments. As an empire they never conquered the land of Canaan itself, although the Hittite local tribes did settle there at an early date. Nothing discovered by the excavators has in any way discredited the Biblical account. Scripture accuracy has once more been proved by the archaeologist.

4 The discovery of the Hittites has proven to be one of the great archaeological finds of all time. It has helped to confirm the biblical narrative and had a great impact on Middle East archaeological study. Because of it, we have come to a greater understanding of the history of our language, as well as the religious, social, and political practices of the ancient Middle East.

This article was taken from *<bible.org>*

Sodom and Gomorrah

The story of Sodom and Gomorrah has long been viewed as a legend. Critics assume that it was created to communicate moral principles. However, throughout the Bible this story is treated as a historical event. The Old Testament prophets refer to the destruction of Sodom on several occasions (Deut. 29:23, Isa. 13:19, Jer. 49:18), and these cities play a key role in the teachings of Jesus and the Apostles (Matt. 10:15, 2 Pet. 2:6 and Jude 1:7). What has archaeology found to establish the existence of these cities?

Archaeologists have searched the Dead Sea region for many years in search of Sodom and Gomorrah. Genesis 14:3 gives their location as the Valley of Siddim known as the Salt Sea, another name for the Dead Sea. On the east side six wadies, or river valleys, flow into the Dead Sea. Along five of these wadies, ancient cities were discovered. The northern most is named Bab edh-Drha. In 1924, renowned archaeologist Dr. William Albright excavated at this site, searching for Sodom and Gomorrah. He discovered it to be a heavily fortified city. Although he connected this city with one of the biblical "Cities of the Plains," he could not find conclusive evidence to justify this assumption.

More digging was done in 1965, 1967, and 1973. The archaeologists discovered a 23-inch thick wall around the city, along with numerous houses and a large temple. Outside the city were huge grave sites where thousands of skeletons were unearthed. This revealed that the city had been well populated during the early Bronze Age, about the time Abraham would have lived.

Most intriguing was evidence that a massive fire had destroyed the city. It lay buried under a coating of ash several feet thick. A cemetery one kilometer outside the city contained charred remains of roofs, posts, and bricks turned red from heat.

Dr. Bryant Wood, in describing these charnel houses, stated that a fire began on the roofs of these buildings. Eventually the burning roof collapsed into the interior and spread inside the building. This was the case in every house they excavated. Such a massive fiery destruction would match the biblical account that the city was destroyed by fire that rained down from heaven. Wood states, "The evidence would suggest that this site of Bab edh-Drha is the biblical city of Sodom."

Five cities of the plain are mentioned in Genesis 14:

Sodom, Gomorrah, Admah, Zoar, and Zeboiim. Remnants of these other four cities are also found along the Dead Sea. Following a southward path from Bab edh-Drha there is the city called Numeria. Continuing south is the city called es-Safi. Further south are the ancient cities of Feifa and Khanazir. Studies at these cities revealed that they had been abandoned at the same time about 2450 2350 B.C. Many archaeologists believe if Bab ed-Drha is Sodom, Numeria is Gomorrah, and es-Safi is Zoar.

What fascinated the archaeologists is that these cities were covered in the same ash as Bab ed-Drha. Numeria, believed to be Gomorrah, had seven feet of ash in some places. In every one of the destroyed cities ash deposits made the soil a spongy charcoal, making it impossible to rebuild. According to the Bible, four of the five cities were destroyed, leaving Lot to flee to Zoar. Zoar was not destroyed by fire, but was abandoned during this period.

Although archaeologists are still disputing these findings, this is one discovery we will be hearing more about in years to come.

Taken from <*bible.org*>

The Walls of Jericho

According to the Bible, the conquest of Jericho occurred in approximately 1440 B.C. The miraculous nature of the conquest has caused some scholars to dismiss the story as folklore. Does archaeology support the biblical account? Over the past century four prominent archaeologists have excavated the site: Carl Watzinger from 1907-1909, John

Garstang in the 1930's, Kathleen Kenyon from 1952-1958, and currently Bryant Wood. The result of their work has been remarkable.

First, they discovered that Jericho had an impressive system of fortifications. Surrounding the city was a retaining wall fifteen feet high. At its top was an eight-foot brick wall strengthened from behind by an earthen rampart. Domestic structures were found behind this first wall. Another brick wall enclosed the rest of the city. The domestic structures found between the two walls is consistent with Joshua's description of Rahab's quarters (Josh. 2:15).

Archeologists also found that in one part of the city, large piles of bricks were found at the base of both the inner and outer walls, indicating a sudden collapse of the fortifications. Scholars feel that an earthquake, which may also explain the damming of the Jordan in the biblical account, caused this collapse. The collapsed bricks formed a ramp by which an invader might easily enter the city (Josh. 6:20).

Of this amazing discovery Garstang states, "As to the main fact, then, there remains no doubt: the walls fell outwards so completely, the attackers would be able to clamber up and over the ruins of the city." This is remarkable because when attacked city walls fall inward, not outward.

A thick layer of soot indicates that the city was destroyed by fire as described in Joshua 6:24. Kenyon describes it this way. "The destruction was complete. Walls and floors were blackened or reddened by fire and every room was filled with fallen bricks." Archaeologists also discovered large amounts of grain at the site. This is again consistent with the biblical account that the city was captured quickly. If it had fallen as a result of a siege, the grain would have been used up. According to Joshua 6:17, the Israelites were forbidden to plunder the city, but had to destroy it totally.

Although the archaeologists agreed Jericho was violently destroyed, they disagreed on the date of the conquest. Garstang held to the biblical date of 1400 B.C. while Watzinger and Kenyon believed the destruction occurred in 1550 B.C. In other words, if the later date is accurate, Joshua arrived at a previously destroyed Jericho. This earlier date would pose a serious challenge to the historicity of the Old Testament.

Dr. Bryant Wood, who is currently excavating the site, found that Kenyon's early date was based on faulty assumptions about pottery found at the site. His later date is also based on the discovery of Egyptian amulets in the tomb's northwest of Jericho. Inscribed under these amulets were the names of Egyptian Pharaohs dating from 1500-1386 B.C., showing that the cemetery was in use up to the end of the late Bronze Age (1550-1400 B.C.). Finally, a piece of charcoal found in the debris was carbon-14 dated to be 1410 B.C. The evidence leads Wood to this conclusion. "The pottery, stratigraphic considerations, scarab data and a carbon-14 date all point to a destruction of the city around the end of the Late Bronze Age, about 1400 BCE."

Thus, current archeological evidence supports the Bible's account of when and how Jericho fell.

The silver Scrolls.

The Ketef Hinnom Silver Scrolls: The Earliest Hebrew Biblical Text and Its Significance for the Authority of the Bible as God's Word

Two small silver scrolls, found in Ketef Hinnom on the western side of Jerusalem, and "dated to the mid-seventh century B. C.," contain parts of Deuteronomy 7:9[2] and Numbers 6:22-27 on two small silver sheets. (When unrolled the larger is about 1 inch wide by 4 inches long and the smaller is about 1/2 inch wide by 1–1/2 inches long).

The scrolls were discovered with other items in the burial cave of a wealthy and prominent family. Pottery in the cave dates as far back as the seventh century, confirming the 7th century date for the scrolls. Furthermore, scroll one's outer edges were worn and split, implying it had been used for a long time before being buried.

Paleography likewise indicates a date between the 9th-7th centuries, and "before the sixth century B.C., hence somewhere in the eighth and seventh." In conclusion, "the convergence of archaeological, paleographic, and orthographic data favors a date around the seventh century B.C. for the composition of this document."

Taken from the site <*faithsaves.net*>

Existence of Edom.

An ancient rival of the Tribe of Judah, the Kingdom of Edom was widely believed to have been an exaggerated myth until modern archaeological discoveries

According to the biblical narrative, Edom was an

ancient kingdom neighboring the Kingdom of Judah. Engaging in sustained conflict with their rivals, the Edomites were supposedly defeated by King Saul, before being subjugated by King David into vassalage. Historical opinion traditionally viewed this claim with great skepticism, with the consensus held that the Edomites, believed to have been a predominantly pastoral civilization, remained too small in size or power to assemble an army as described. However, modern archaeological explorations have greatly expanded the potential scale of the ancient kingdom and offered tacit corroboration.

Discoveries at the Khirbat en-Nahas archaeological site have concluded that the Kingdom of Edom was not merely a pastoral society but instead one chiefly focused on copper mining. Slag heaps, pottery, and even an Iron Age fortress, dated to around the 10th century BCE, all demonstrate the long-standing existence of a far more advanced and militarized civilization. Further adding to the historicity of the biblical story, reference is made to an Egyptian ruler who invaded the area in the years after the death of Soloman to claim the resources of Edom. Recent archaeological surveys have uncovered an ancient Egyptian amulet in modern-day Jordan, inscribed with the name of Pharaoh Shesong.

Solomons Wall around Jerusalem

Long thought to have been an invention of an imaginative author, the discovery of Solomon's Walls in Jerusalem has renewed speculation concerning other biblical wonders

According to the First Book of Kings, Soloman, the son of David and King of Judah, at some time after marrying the daughter of the Egyptian Pharaoh ordered the construction of a great wall around the ancient city of Jerusalem. Written many centuries after the alleged event, and with no corroborating evidence of the defensive structure's existence, the historical consensus was that it did not exist and, as is common throughout scripture, was merely allegorical.

Demonstrating that the absence of evidence cannot be taken for certain as evidence of absence, modern archaeological excavations led by Eilat Mazar proved otherwise.

Measuring approximately 70 meters in length and 6 meters high, these ancient remains situate the wall's location precisely encompass the best estimates of the city of Jerusalem during this time. Including a gatehouse and guard tower, the purpose of the structure as one for military defense is indisputable. Helping to date the remains of the ancient wall, remnants of pottery from the late-10th century BCE, the reign of Solomon, help corroborate the contextuality of the structure. Providing the first evidence of Soloman's great building works, the discovery of the wall has renewed speculation regarding other attributed projects including the First Temple.

Taken from <*historycollection.com*>

Isaiah. Among the oldest pieces of physical proof for any individual appearing in the Bible, an ancient seal bearing the name of the Prophet Isaiah strongly indicates the physical existence of a correlatory figure.

Isaiah, an 8th-century BCE prophet commonly ascribed authorship of the eponymous sixty-six chapter book of the Bible, remains a highly disputed figure within the biblical narrative. Living supposedly during the reigns of Uzziah, Jotham, Ahaz, and Hezekiah, who reigned as Kings of Judah between the mid-8th century and the late-7th century, Isaiah, however, enjoys no corroborating reference in any alternative historical sources reducing his story that of considerable skepticism. Despite this doubt regarding the veracity of his legend, Isaiah most likely did exist and remains the most ancient biblical character for whom archaeological evidence has been discovered concerning.

In the course of an archaeological excavation in Jerusalem, in a stroke of luck, a small clay seal dating to the 8th-century BCE was discovered. Although surviving only partially, upon the ancient artifact is inscribed the name "Yesha'yahu" – Isaiah in Hebrew – and is followed by what is believed to be the beginning of the ancient Hebrew word for prophet: "Nvy…" The conclusion one must reach from this historic find is that, although by no means confirming anything stated in the Book of Isaiah, that an individual in a position of religious significance bearing his name almost certainly did exist around this time.

Taken from <historycollection.com>

Gilgamesh

In 1872, George Smith announced he had discovered an Assyrian account of a flood among tablets stored in the British Museum from excavations of mid-seventh-century-BC Nineveh. Called the Epic of Gilgamesh, the story comprises twelve tablets, with one tablet containing a tale of a great deluge. The hero of the flood, a man named Utnapishtim, relates an episode to Gilgamesh. He explains how the god Ea warned him about an approaching judgment and told him to build a boat to save his life from the watery onslaught. As the tale unfolds, the epic in some respects is nearly identical to the biblical narrative of Noah in Genesis 6–9. This discovery created quite a stir among biblical scholars of the nineteenth century, and even today scholars continue to puzzle over and debate the obvious parallels between the two.

Taken from <crossway.com>

Hezekiah's tunnel.

The most dependable water source for the city of Jerusalem during the Israelite settlement was the Gihon Spring. However, its location outside the city walls was problematic. During an attack or siege, the inhabitants were cut off from their vital water source. In 1867, explorer Charles Warren discovered a vertical shaft cut through bedrock allowing the people of Jerusalem to reach the waters of the Gihon Spring from behind the city walls. This shaft was probably built originally by the Jebusites and may be how David's soldiers captured the city from them (2 Sam. 5:6–8). A new water system employing part of the earlier one was built by Hezekiah near the end of the eighth century BC due to an Assyrian military threat. Hezekiah's tunnel sloped gently away from the Gihon Spring to allow water to flow from it to the Pool of Siloam inside the city walls.

Hezekiah's tunnel was cut by two teams digging toward each other from opposite ends. It was not chiseled in a straight line but was serpentine due to frequent shifts in terrain. The two teams made adjustments as they drew near each other and heard the picks of the other team. An inscription twenty feet (six meters) from the Siloam Pool has been discovered that describes the meeting of the two cutting teams.

Taken from <crossway.org>

The Moabite Stone.

In 1868, a missionary in Jerusalem found a stone tablet for sale that appeared to be from ancient times. The sellers broke the tablet into a number of pieces to sell them one at a time to make more money. Fortunately, a copy of the tablet was made prior to the break (this copy is in the Louvre today). On the tablet is a text written in Moabite dating to the ninth century BC. It was perhaps a victory stone erected by King Mesha to commemorate his military achievements. The text begins, "I am Mesha son of Chemosh, king of Moab."

Prominent in the text is the king's version of a war fought with Israel in 850 BC, in which Moab revolted against King Jehoram of the northern kingdom of Israel soon after the death of Ahab. Of particular interest is that the Bible records the same incident in 2 Kings 3. The two accounts differ in perspective. Mesha emphasizes his victories over Israel in capturing cities under Israelite control. The biblical writer, to the contrary, highlights Israel's successful counter attacks against the Moabites.

Taken from <crossway.org>

The Cyrus cylinder.

One of the most famous artifacts in biblical archaeology is undoubtedly the Cyrus Cylinder. Sometimes hailed as the first declaration of human rights, a copy of it resides in the headquarters of the United Nations. More to the point of this blog, the Cyrus Cylinder confirms the biblical claim that Cyrus allowed the Jewish people who had been captured by the Babylonians to return to their homeland and rebuild their temple.

The Cyrus Cylinder was discovered in 1879 in the ruins of Babylon by Hormuzd Rassam. It is a baked clay cylinder, measuring 22.5cm by 10cm. and inscribed in Akkadian cuneiform script. It contains a general declaration by Cyrus the Great stating;

I sent back to their places...whose shrines had earlier become dilapidated, the gods who lived therein, and made permanent sanctuaries for them. I collected all their peoples and returned them to their settlements...I returned them unharmed to their cells, in the sanctuaries that make them happy. May all the gods that I returned to their sanctuaries, every day before Bel and Nabu, ask for a long life for me, and mention my good deeds.

The inscription confirms Cyrus' general policy of returning exiles to their "settlements" and allowing them to take their gods with them and rebuild their "sanctuaries." The Jewish people had no idols, so the articles that had been taken from the Temple were returned. Cyrus' specific proclamation for the Jews is recorded in Ezra 1:1-3:

In the first year of Cyrus king of Persia, that the word of the LORD by the mouth of Jeremiah might be fulfilled, the LORD stirred up the spirit of Cyrus king of Persia, so that he made a proclamation throughout all his kingdom and also put it in writing: "Thus says Cyrus king of Persia: The LORD, the God of heaven, has given me all the kingdoms of the earth, and he has charged me to build him a house at Jerusalem, which is in Judah. Whoever is among you of all his people, may his God be with him, and let him go up to Jerusalem, which is in Judah, and rebuild the house of the LORD, the God of Israel—he is the God who is in Jerusalem.

Ezra further records that "Cyrus the king also brought out the vessels of the house of the LORD that Nebuchadnezzar had carried away from Jerusalem and placed in the house of his gods"

While 19th century skeptics had scoffed at the biblical claim that a king would allow captured people to return to their homes and rebuild their temples, the Cyrus Cylinder confirms that this was indeed the policy of Cyrus the Great.

Taken from <*biblearchaeologyreport.com*>

Mernepth Stele.

The Hebrew Bible records that throughout their history the Israelites and Egyptians had significant interactions on numerous occasions. But is there any evidence of this from the Egyptian side?

In 1896, Sir Flinders Petrie discovered a huge 10-foot-tall inscribed monument – called a stele – that recounted the victories of the ancient Egyptian Pharaoh, Merneptah, who reigned from 1213 to 1203 BC. Known as the Merneptah Stele, or the Victory Stele of Merneptah, it is an account of his victories over the Libyans. The last three lines on the Stele, however, deal with a separate campaign into Canaan. There we read, "Israel is wasted, its seed is not. "While Merneptah is claiming to have destroyed Israel, we know from the Bible and other historical records that this did not happen. In fact, Israel continued to live and prosper in Canaan for the next 600 years!

Still, the Merneptah stele is an important discovery in biblical archaeology for several reasons:

First, is the oldest definitive reference to Israel as a nation outside of the Bible.

Second, it's the clearest Egyptian reference to Israel as a nation.

And thirdly, it confirms the chronology of the Bible. According to clues in 1 Kings 6:1, the exodus from Egypt took place in the year 1446 BC, not 1270 BC as some have claimed. After wandering in the desert for 40 years, the Israelites eventually reached the promised land and began the conquest of Canaan, a process that took years. The Merpentan Stele itself dates to around 1205-1210 BC, and supports the early date for the exodus. There simply isn't enough time from 1270 BC to 1210 BC for the exodus, the 40 years of wandering in the desert, the conquest of Canaan, and the establishment of the nation of Israel there before Merpentan claims to have conquered them. Rather Merneptah's campaign dates to the time of the Judges, when Israel was already settled in Canaan.

Taken from *<biblearchaeologyreport.com>*

The "Jerusalem Chronicle" (Babylonian

Chronicle, 605-595 BC)

The Babylonian Chronicles are a series of clay tablets held by the British Museum that recount the history of the kings of Babylon. The Babylonian Chronicle for the years 605-594 BC records the fall of Jerusalem under Nebuchadnezzar (hence it's nickname – the Jerusalem Chronicle). It reads: "Year 7 [597 BC] in Kislev the king of Babylonia [Nebuchadnezzar] called out his army and marched to Hattu [the west]. He set his camp against the city of Judah and on the second Adar [March 16] he took the city and captured the king [Jehoiachin]. He appointed a king of his choosing there [Zedekiah], took heavy tribute, and returned to Babylon"

This account refers to the second deportation of the Hebrews in 597 BC (the first being in 605 BC when Daniel and his friends were taken to Babylon). It confirms the biblical description of Nebuchadnezzar's siege and eventual capture of Jerusalem (2 Kings 24:10), the deportation of King Jehoiachin (2 Kings 24:15), the appointment of a new King (Zedekiah – 2 Kings 24:17), and the heavy tribute taken back to Babylon (the treasures of the Temple and the treasures of the kings – 2 Chron. 36:18).

Chapter 4

Examples from Astronomy

We read in the Bible that the stars in the heavens and the sands on the sea shore cannot be numbered.

Jeremiah 33:22, As the host of heaven cannot be numbered, neither the sand of the sea measured: so will I multiply the seed of David my servant, and the Levites that minister unto me.

The first recorded information on man's knowledge of the stars in heaven was from Hipparchus. He listed 850 stars with their position in the sky. His information was then handed down to Ptolemy, who increased that amount to 1025. The timing of Hipparchus star count was between 162 and 127 BC.

As we follow this thread we find the number of stars increases with the invention of the telescope and the subsequent improvements. The first telescope was invented in 1680 AD. The time frame of the book of Jeremiah was 586-538 BCE. That means that the time between Jeremiah's writing and the first counting of the stars was 411 years. At that point, man thought he could count all the stars. The time from Jeremiah's writing and the first telescope was over 2000 years. How could Jeremiah know that the stars could not be numbered? We can answer that with the following verse.

2 Peter 1:21 For the prophecy came not in old time by the

will of man: but holy men of God spake as they were moved by the Holy Ghost.

Jeremiah could have only known that the stars could not be counted through the omniscience of God. That should be enough, by itself, to make one realize that the Bible is the Word of God.

As the telescope has improved over time, it has become evident that we cannot count the stars. The Hubble telescope, in use now, is the latest improvement to its evolution, as you can see from the following information, we still don't know how many stars there are in the universe. Our Galaxy alone is thought to contain 100 billion stars.

A gentleman by the name of David Kornreich used a very rough estimate of 10 trillion galaxies in the universe. Multiplying that by the Milky Way's estimated 100 billion stars results in a very large number indeed: 1,000,000,000, 000,000,000,000,000 stars, or a "1" with 24 zeros after it (1 septillion in the American numbering system; 1 quadrillion in the European system). David Kornreich emphasized that the number is likely a gross underestimation, as a more detailed observations of the universe, with stronger telescopes, will show even more galaxies.

How long would it take for a person to count all those stars? I believe that is too many stars to count. Today we still do not know how many stars there are as we have no idea what we will discover as the telescope continues to be improved.

Do you believe now that the Bible is the Word of God? Not enough proof for you yet, then let's continue.

Stars can move relative to each other.

Job 38:31: *"Can you bind the cluster of the Pleiades, or loose the belt of Orion?"*

Who wrote this, and when was the Book of Job written? There are several different times suggested. I provide the following information.

Job was a real person as Ezekiel 14:14–20 (KJV) and James 5:11 (KJV) indicate. He was a native of the land of Uz (Job 1: 19 KJV), which scholars have located either northeast of Palestine near desert land, probably between the city of Damascus and the Euphrates River, or to the southeast in the area of Edom. Job probably lived before or around the time of Abraham (c. 2167–1992 BC).

Both Ptolemy and Copernicus took for granted that the stars were fixed in place. Although God's point was to remind Job of His infinite power, not to teach him astronomy, He implied that the stars are not anchored to their positions! Job 38:31 suggests correctly that stars can move; they can draw together or drift apart.

The constellations God mentions are among the best visible examples of both phenomena. The Pleiades are a close-knit group of hundreds of stars called an open cluster, held together by gravitational attraction. Yet gravity can also throw stars out of an open cluster. That is to say, the Pleiades are tenuously bound, as the Bible suggests.

In contrast, the three points of light in Orion's belt appear to be a unit, but each has a different trajectory. Eventually, as astronomer Garrett P. Serviss projected in 1909, "the two right-hand stars, Mintaka and Alnilam will approach each other and form a naked-eye double, but the third, Alnita [also known as Alnitak], will drift away eastward so that the 'Belt' will no longer exist. In other words, Orion's belt is loosening!

Yet part of the "belt" is tightly bound: Alnitak is a triple star, three stars bound by gravity in orbits more stable than an open cluster. The Bible hinted at these dynamic interactions among stars long before humans had the technology to detect them!

For nearly 1,000 years, Aristotle's view of a stationary Earth at the center of a revolving universe dominated natural philosophy, the name that scholars, of that time, used for studies of the physical world. A geocentric worldview became ingrained in Christian theology, making it a doctrine of religion as much as natural philosophy. Despite that, it was a priest who brought back the idea that the Earth moves around the Sun.

In 1515, a Polish priest named Nicolaus Copernicus proposed that the Earth was a planet like Venus or Saturn, and that all planets circled the Sun. Afraid of criticism (some scholars think Copernicus was more concerned about scientific shortcomings of his theories than he was about the Church's disapproval), he did not publish his theory until 1543, shortly before his death. The theory gathered few followers, and for a time, some of those who did give credence to the idea faced charges of heresy. Italian scientist Giordano Bruno was burned at the stake for teaching Copernicus' theory, among other heretical ideas,

If you add the 1900 years BC that Job was written with the 1500 years AD that Copernicus suggested that the planets orbited the sun, you get over 3000 years. Let me ask you this, how could the writer of Job have known this? Because man was moved by the Holy Spirit to write the Word of God. The Bible **is** God's Word.

Earths Shape

Isaiah 40:22 It is he that sitteth upon the circle of the earth, and the inhabitants thereof are as grasshoppers; that stretcheth out the heavens as a curtain, and spreadeth them out as a tent to dwell in:

In this verse God is telling Isaiah that He is the one that created earth, and that He is the one controlling it as He sits above the vault of the earth, not the idols made by the hands of man. I believe that this is the main purpose of this verse. However, because God created the earth He also knew it is spherical in shape. Just because the people of that time thought the earth was flat does not mean that God would describe it as thus. He would not tell you something that was not true. So, He gave us a clue to the shape of the earth for those who would seek the Holy Spirit's guiding in this matter.

Who was the first to declare that the earth was a sphere?

<*Alabasterco.com*> gives the following information on the above question. It was Pythagoras who first proposed that the earth was round in 500 BC. He reached this conclusion by observing the terminator (the line between the part of the moon in light and the part of the moon in the dark) as it moved through its orbital cycle. That and the shape of the earth's shadow on the moon, during a lunar eclipse, it was also used as evidence that Earth was round, as noted by Anaxagoras later.

So, from the time of the writing of Isaiah, around 740 BC, the earliest proof that stated the Earth was a sphere, came in 500 BC. That it was approximately 240 years between the writing of Isaiah and the later proof stated by Pythagoras. How could the writer of Isaiah know this 240 years before man learned it?

2 Peter 1:20, 21 *Knowing this first, that no prophecy of the scripture is of any private interpretation.*

21For the prophecy came not in old time by the will of man: but holy men of God spake as they were moved by the Holy Ghost.

What you read in the Bible is directly from God. The Bible **IS** God's Word.

The earth is suspended on nothing

Job 26:7 He stretcheth out the north over the empty place, and hangeth the earth upon nothing.

When and who wrote the Book of Job? There is no specific answer to this question; but several commentators suggest that Moses was the author. If that is the case Moses lived in the 14th and 15th centuries BC.

Who then proved that Earth is suspended in space? There is no single person this can be attributed to. It was people like Brahe, Newton, and Kepler, that contributed to that theory. However, it was not until the Russian satellite Sputnik was launched that proved there were no lines, poles, or any other sources holding the earth in place, only gravity. That took place in 1957.

If you then take the time Job was written, 1500BC added to the 1900 years that sputnik was launched you get a total of 3457 years. How then did the writer of Job know this? God wrote the Bible through holy men led by the Holy Spirit. The Bible is the Word of God.

35

Second Law of Thermodynamics

Psalm 102:25,26: *"Of old You founded the earth, and the heavens are the work of Your hands. Even they will perish, but You endure; and all of them will wear out like a garment"* (NASB).

The Bible tells us three times that the earth is wearing out like a garment. This is the Second Law of Thermodynamics. (the Law of Increasing Entropy) states: that all physical processes, every ordered system, over time, become more disordered.

Everything is running down and wearing out as energy is becoming less and less available for use. That means the universe will eventually "wear out"—something that wasn't discovered by science until fairly recently. The first rigorous definition of the second law based on the concept of entropy came from German scientist Rudolf Clausius in the 1850s AD. Psalm 102 was written in 538BC per the Blue Line Bible. That is 2388 years before the second law was defined. How could the author of Ps.102 know this?

Hydrology Cycle

Amos 9:6 (written 2,800 years ago): *It is he that buildeth his stories in the heaven, and hath founded his troop in the earth; he that calleth for the waters of the sea, and poureth them out upon the face of the earth: The LORD is his name.*

The Mississippi River dumps over six million gallons of water per second into the Gulf of Mexico. Where does all that water go? That is just one of thousands of rivers. The answer lies in the hydrology cycle—something not fully understood until the 17th century, but so well brought out in the Bible.

Ecclesiastes 1:7 *All the rivers run into the sea; yet the sea is not full; unto the place from whence the rivers come, thither they return again.*

Psalm 135:7 *"He causes the vapors to ascend from the ends of the earth; He makes lightning for the rain."*

Ecclesiastes 11:3 *"if the clouds are full of rain, they empty themselves upon the earth."*

It took well over 2000 years for a reasonable understanding of the science of hydrology to evolve. Not until the pioneering work of John Dalton in about 1800 were all the mechanisms of the large-scale hydrological cycle properly determined.

The Science of Oceanography

Psalm 8:8: *"...and the fish of the sea that pass through the paths of the seas."*

The sea is just a huge mass of water; how could it have "paths"? Man discovered the existence of ocean currents in the 1850s, but the Bible declared the science of oceanography 2,800 years prior. Matthew Maury (1806–1873), considered the father of oceanography, noticed the expression "paths of the sea" in Psalm 8. Maury took God at His word and went looking for these paths, and his vital book on oceanography is still in print today.

Job 26:8 *He wraps up the waters in his clouds, yet the clouds do not burst under their weight.*

Job 36:27-28 *27For he maketh small the drops of water: they pour down rain according to the vapour thereof:*

28Which the clouds do drop and distil upon man abundantly.

"wraps up the waters" : evaporation
"Distill upon man" : precipitation
"Clouds do drop" : condensation

The first published thinker to assert that rainfall alone was sufficient for the maintenance of rivers was Bernard Palissy (1580 CE), who is often credited as the "discoverer" of the modern theory of the water cycle. Palissy's theories were not tested scientifically until 1674,

Life is in the Blood

Leviticus 17:11 *"For the life of the flesh is in the blood: and I have given it to you upon the altar to make an atonement for your souls: for it is the blood that maketh an atonement for the soul."*

This great verse contains a wealth of scientific and spiritual truth. It was not realized until the discovery of the circulation of the blood by the creation scientist William Harvey, in about 1620, that biological "life" really is maintained by the blood, which both brings nourishment to all parts of the body and carries away its wastes.

Its spiritual truth is even more significant. The blood, when shed on the altar, would serve as an "atonement" (literally "covering") for the soul of the guilty sinner making the offering. The "life" of the flesh is its "soul," for "life" and "soul" both translate the same Hebrew word (nephesh) in this text. When the blood was offered, it was thus an offering of life itself in substitution for the life of the sinner who deserved to die.

Human sacrifices, of course, were prohibited. No man could die for another man, for his blood would inevitably be contaminated by his sin. Therefore, the blood of a "clean animal" was required. Animals do not possess the "image of God" (Genesis 1:27), including the ability to reason about right and wrong, and therefore cannot sin. Even such clean blood could only serve as a temporary covering, and it could not "take away" sin. For a permanent solution to the sin problem, nothing less was required than that of a sinless person.

John 1:29 *The next day John seeth Jesus coming unto him, and saith, Behold the Lamb of God, which taketh away the sin of the world.*

Hebrews 9:12 *"Neither by the blood of goats and calves, but by his own blood he entered in once into the holy place, having obtained eternal redemption for us."*

Since His life was in His blood, (Jesus) He has "made peace through His blood shed on the cross."

I could give numerous other examples, but if you cannot see, from the above examples, I do not think more examples are going to convince you that the Bible is Gods Word. Do your own research. Just type in, Bible verses that science has proven to be true.

Chapter 5

Other Examples

What is meant by the phrase "fine-tuned universe"?

"Fine-tuning" refers to various features of the universe that are necessary conditions for the existence of complex life. Such features include the initial conditions and "brute facts" of the universe as a whole, the laws of nature or the numerical constants present in those laws (such as the gravitational force constant), and local features of habitable planets (such as a planet's distance from its host star). The basic idea is that these features must fall within a very narrow range of possible values for chemical-based life to be possible.

Some popular examples are subject to dispute. There are some complicated philosophical debates about how to calculate probabilities. Nevertheless, there are many well-established examples of fine-tuning, which are widely accepted even by scientists who are generally hostile to theism and design. For instance, Stephen Hawking has admitted: "The remarkable fact is that the values of these numbers [the constants of physics] seem to have been very finely adjusted to make possible the development of life."

Here are the most celebrated and widely accepted examples of fine-tuning for the existence of life: Cosmic Constants

(1)   Gravitational force constant

(2)   Electromagnetic force constant

(3)   Strong nuclear force constant

(4)   Weak nuclear force constant

(5)   Cosmological constant

Explanation of each constant.

(1)   Gravitational force constant (large scale attractive force, holds people on planets, and holds planets, stars, and galaxies together)—too weak, and planets and stars cannot form; too strong, and stars burn up too quickly.

(2)   Electromagnetic force constant (small scale attractive and repulsive force, holds atoms electrons and atomic nuclei together)—If it were much stronger or weaker, we would not have stable chemical bonds.

(3)   Strong nuclear force constant (small-scale attractive force, holds nuclei of atoms together, which otherwise repulse each other because of the electromagnetic force)—if it were weaker, the universe would have far fewer stable chemical elements, eliminating several that are essential to life.

(4)   Weak nuclear force constant (governs radioactive decay)—if it were much stronger or weaker, life-essential stars could not form. (These are the four "fundamental forces.") 286

(5)   Cosmological constant (which controls the expansion speed of the universe) refers to the balance of the attractive force of gravity with a hypothesized repulsive force of space observable only at very large

size scales. It must be very close to zero, that is, these two forces must be nearly perfectly balanced.

To get the right balance, the cosmological constant must be fine-tuned to something like 1 part in 10^{120}. If it were just slightly more positive, the universe would fly apart; slightly negative, and the universe would collapse. As with the cosmological constant, the ratios of the other constants must be fine-tuned relative to each other.

Since the logically-possible range of strengths of some forces is potentially infinite, to get a handle on the precision of fine-tuning, theorists often think in terms of the range of force strengths, with gravity the weakest, and the strong nuclear force the strongest. The strong nuclear force is 10^{40} times stronger than gravity, that is, ten thousand, billion, billion, billion, billion times the strength of gravity. Think of that range as represented by a ruler stretching across the entire observable universe, about 15 billion light years. If we increased the strength of gravity by just 1 part in 10^{34} of the range of force strengths (the equivalent of moving less than one inch on the universe-long ruler), the universe could not have life-sustaining planets.

Fine-tuning arguments look at factors that influence the nature of the universe. According to the fine-tuning argument, the exact quantity of each physical constant and the respective ratios must all be precisely as they are for life to exist on Earth. In most cases, the tiniest change to one of these constants would not only prohibit life as we know it, but it would make most forms of matter impossible, as well. Our universe is not merely tuned to allow for "some kind" of life, but it seems to be arranged in the only way that allows for "any life," at all. For me, this fine-tuning gives evidence for a creator.

Theologians were ecstatic when physicists started talking about the fine-tuned universe. Believers now had a scientific angle, with which to use as evidence of a creator. Apologists, like William Lane Craig, use the fine-tuned universe in arguments for a creator.

An example of fine-tuning that is cited by apologists, is the calculation for life randomly forming on Earth. Using a self-replicating peptide model that is 32 amino acids long, the odds of it forming randomly, were 1 in 10^{40}. Other models have calculated 1 in 10^{45}. That is 1 in 10 with 45 zeroes behind it.

This is what it looks like:

1 in 10,000,000,000,000,000,000,000,000,
00 0,000,000,000,000,000,000

Practically impossible, yet, here we are. The question then becomes, given those odds, did the fine-tuning occur naturally, or was there some type of Providence behind it?

Here are four classic examples from Robin Collins,

1. If the initial explosion of the big bang had differed in strength by as little as one part in 10^{60}, the universe would have either quickly collapsed back on itself, or expanded too rapidly for stars to form. In either case, life would be impossible.

2. (As John Jefferson Davis points out, an accuracy of one part in 10^{60} can be compared to firing a bullet at a one-inch target on the other side of the

observable universe, twenty billion light years away, and hitting the target.)

3. Calculations by Brandon Carter show that if gravity had been stronger or weaker by one part in 10^40, then life-sustaining stars like the sun could not exist. This would most likely make life impossible.

4. As the Earth moves in its orbit around the Sun, it departs from a straight line by only one-ninth of an inch every eighteen miles. If it departed by one-eighth of an inch, we would come so close to the Sun that we would be incinerated; if it departed by one-tenth of an inch, we would find ourselves so far from the Sun that we would all freeze to death.

Another finely tuned constant is the strong nuclear force (the force that holds atoms together). The Sun "burns" by fusing hydrogen (and higher elements) together. When the two hydrogen atoms fuse, 0.7% of the mass of the hydrogen is converted into energy. If the amount of matter converted were slightly smaller—0.6% instead of 0.7%—a proton could not bond to a neutron, and the universe would consist only of hydrogen. With no heavy elements, there would be no rocky planets and no life. If the amount of matter converted were slightly larger—0.8%, fusion would happen so readily and rapidly that no hydrogen would have survived from the Big Bang. Again, there would be no solar systems and no life. The number must lie exactly between 0.6% and 0.8%.

The probabilities involved with the fine-tuning of the universe are not comparable to winning the lottery or being struck by lightning. Lottery odds are represented using eight or nine digits, e.g., 1:109. Randomly dealing a deck of 52 playing cards in perfect order presents odds of 1:1068. Physicists express the odds of "randomly" arranging universal physical constants in the present arrangement using numbers more like 1:10120.

In that sense, a universe capable of sustaining intelligent life is like a treasure hidden in a safe whose dial has millions of numbers and whose proper combination is millions of digits long. A single wrong digit, anywhere, and there is no result. It cannot be partly opened, or mostly opened—the door is entirely closed unless the combination is perfect.

If someone opened that million-digit lock, it would be overwhelmingly likely they did so on purpose. Immediately dismissing the feat as random chance would be inane. Lacking any evidence that the person repeated random digits until the safe opened. The most sensible conclusion is "fine-tuning."

Fine-tuning points to specific properties of the universe and posits that some higher power deliberately chose their arrangement. This is grounded in a reasonable assumption, based on the evidence at hand. Of course, as with the cosmological argument, the fine-tuning argument gives little information about the nature of the "Fine-tuner."

One reaction to these apparent enormous coincidences is to see them as substantiating the theistic claim that the universe has been created by a personal God and as offering the material for a properly restrained theistic argument—hence the fine-tuning argument. It is as if there are a large number of dials that have to be tuned to within extremely narrow limits for life to be possible in our universe. It is extremely unlikely that this should happen by chance, but much more likely that this should happen, if there is such a person as God.

If you would like to explore this subject further, type into your search engine the following, "What Does the Bible Say about the Big Bang?" or (what does the Bible say about fine-tuning In section chapter six you will see what (I assume.) You will find numerous articles on the subject.

SECTION TWO
The Guide To Eternal Life

Chapter 6

Man's Nature

Gen. 1:26 *And God said, Let Us make man in Our Image, after Our likeness and let them have dominion over the fish of the sea, and over the fowl of the air, and over the cattle, and over all the earth, and over every creeping thing that creeps upon the Earth.*

When God created man, He made him a perfect being. He was in the continual presence of God and He was placed in the Garden of Eden to take care of it.

Gen 2:15 *And the Lord God took the man, and put him in the Garden of Eden to dress it and to keep it.*

Man was created to live forever in the presence of God and to have dominion over all the Earth.

However, there were some rules to this existence. Man was not to eat from the Tree of Knowledge of good and evil. If he did he would die.

Gen. 2:17 *But of the tree of the Knowledge of Good and Evil, you shall not eat of it for in the day you eat thereof you shall surely die.*

We all know the story from here. The serpent beguiled Eve, Adam's wife, and after eating the fruit of the Garden and finding it to be good she gave some to Adam and he ate it. Immediately they were separated from the presence of God, (spiritual death) and they hid in the bushes. Man, also lost his eternal physical life.

Heb. 9:27 *And it is appointed for men once to die, but after this the judgment.*

This verse tells us our days are now numbered because Adam sinned, sin then passes to our children. The following scriptures tell us that everyone born inherits a sinful nature.

Romans 5:12 *"Wherefore, as by one man sin entered into the world, and death by sin; and so death passed upon all men, for that all have sinned:"*

You can do a little experiment to prove this. Get a playpen, place two toddlers in the playpen, and put one rubber ducky in with them. I can guarantee you that they will fight each other to play with it. They cannot help it; they have a sinful nature. You must teach a child to be good but not to be bad, that comes naturally. It also tells you that sin not only affected us, it also affected all of creation.

Romans 8:22 *For we know that the whole creation groaneth and travaileth in pain together until now.*

Some other examples in scripture telling us that we are sinful.

Rom. 3:23 *For all have sinned and come short of the glory of God.*

Rom. 3:10-12 *As it is written, there is none righteous, no not one. There is none who understands, there is none who seek after God. They have all gone out of the way, they are altogether become unprofitable; there is none who does good, no, not one.*

Is there any doubt about what man is? he is a sinner who seeks his own pleasures instead of God's ways. Where does that leave you?

What is Your Future as a Sinner?

Rom. 5:12 *Wherefore, as by one man sin entered into the world, and death by sin; and so death passed upon all men, for that all have sinned:*

Rom. 6:23 *For the wages of sin is death, but the gift of God is eternal life in Christ Jesus our Lord.*

What these two scriptures tell us is that we all face spiritual and physical death. At this point many people say, that if I am good enough, go to church regularly, if I read my bible, pray, and treat my fellow man with respect, maybe I will make it to heaven. What does the Bible tell us about that way of thinking?

Rom. 2:8,9 *For by grace you are saved by faith, and that not of yourselves: It is the gift of God: Not of works, lest any man should boast.*

Isa. 64:6 *But we are like an unclean thing, and all our righteousnesses are like filthy rags;*

This tells us that there is absolutely nothing we can do to gain eternal life on our own. Our very best is as filthy rags in His eyes. We are eternally doomed to eternal death. I can think of nothing that could be worse than to be sentenced to eternal torment in the depths of Hell, and that is exactly where the Word of God tells us we are heading if we try to do it our way.

What have we learned from this chapter?

1. That we are all sinners and have come short of the glory of God.
2. That the penalty for sin is death, both physical and spiritual.
3. There is nothing we can do, in and of ourselves, to save ourselves or to gain eternal life.

There you have it; we are all sinners and on the road to a future we cannot change ourselves. So, what can we do? Where do we go from here?

Chapter 7

Gods Answer

John 3:16 *For God so loved the world that He gave His only begotten Son, that whoever believes in Him should not perish but have everlasting life.*

This verse says more about God and how He feels about us than any other verse in the Bible. He sacrificed His only son so we could have forgiveness of sin and eternal life with Him. Jesus paid the penalty for our sins which we could not do ourselves.

Rom. 5:9 *Much more then, having been justified by His blood, we shall be saved from the wrath of God through Him.*

God's plan of salvation began when Adam and Eve sinned in the Garden of Eden. Adam was created in God's image, in other words, he was a perfect being. While Adam was a perfect being, he had free will. Why would God give Adam, and us, free will? Because He wanted man to love Him because man wanted to. Would you want your children or wife or parents to love you if they had no choice or would you rather, they loved you because they wanted to?

Then Adam disobeyed God and sinned by eating the fruit from the Tree of Knowledge of good and evil. God was not surprised by this and stressing over it. Remember God is Omniscient, He knows everything, past, present, and future. He knew man would sin. Nothing that happens, good or bad, surprises God. So, before He created the heavens and the earth, He knew that Adam would sin and He formulated a plan of salvation for humanity.

I Peter 1:20 *He indeed was foreordained before the foundation of the world, but was manifest in these last times for you.*

This is what John 3:16 is all about. God sent His Son, Jesus Christ, to shed His blood on Calvary's cross to be the perfect sacrifice and pay the penalty for our sin and sins. Our "Sin" is the inherited sin nature we received from Adam; our "sins" are the ones we make daily throughout our lives.

When the people of Israel offered an animal for sacrifice, it had to be perfect, without blemish, a picture of the Messiah to come.

The Israelites had to sacrifice animals to have communion with God. You cannot stand before God with sin in your heart.

In Heb. 9:22 we read *"without shedding of blood is no remission of sin.*

Their sacrifices were only a temporary atonement.

Heb. 10:4 *For it is not possible that the blood of bulls and goats could take away sin.*

These sacrifices had to be repeated over and over. They were a picture of the coming Messiah who would shed His blood for us once and for all time. There had to be a perfect man to shed his blood to pay the penalty for our sins. Since there were no perfect men, God had to send His Son Jesus Christ to accomplish this. The only way our sins could be atoned for was to have a perfect human pay the penalty for our sins.

The Messiah, of the Old Testament, came to earth with the birth of Jesus. John the Baptist said when he saw Jesus coming to him in the wilderness.

John 1:29 *"Behold! The Lamb of God who takes away the sins of the world!*

Jesus came to earth being 100% God and 100% man. While He was on the earth He laid aside his Godly powers and lived for 33 ½ years as a perfect man. From the day He was born until the day He died, on the cross, He never sinned.

God's Son, Jesus was that perfect sacrifice. Jesus was tempted just like you and I but never sinned. To be a sacrifice for us He had to be sinless. This is the reason He had to be born of a virgin so He would not have the inherited sin of His human father. His entire purpose was to go to the cross of Calvary and be crucified, shed His blood, and pay the penalty for all our sins. That is love in its purest form.

Eph. 1:7 *In him we have redemption through His blood, the forgiveness of sins, according to the riches of His grace.*

When we accept Jesus, not only are our sins forgiven they are completely forgotten by God the Father.

Ps. 103:12 *As far as the East is from the West, so far has He removed our transgression from us.*

Heb. 8:12 *"For I will be merciful to their unrighteousness, and their sins and their lawless deeds' I will remember no more."*

What have we learned in this chapter?

1. We are all sinners.

   Rom. 3:23 *For all have sinned and fall short of the glory of God.*

2. The wages of sin is death. Both physical and spiritual death.

   Rom. 6:23 *For the wages of sin is death, but the gift of God is eternal life in Christ Jesus our Lord.*

3. We are unable to escape the wages of sin on our own. God alone provided a way for us to have eternal life with Him.

   Rom. 2:8,9 *For by grace are you saved by faith! And that not of yourselves: It is the gift of God: Not of works, lest any man should boast.*

4. Jn. 14:6 *Jesus said to him, I am the way, the truth, and the life. No man comes unto to the Father except through Me.*

   Jesus and Jesus alone was able and did pay the penalty for our sin and sin's. In Him alone is our salvation.

Chapter 8

Man's Responsibility

In the past two chapters, we have learned that we are sinners and on the road to eternal damnation and there is nothing we can do about it. We also learned that God has provided a way to escape this dilemma.

In this chapter, we will learn how we can claim God's plan and gain eternal life with Him for eternity.

Question, who can claim God's way of escape?

Rom. 10:13 *For whosoever shall call upon the name of the Lord shall be saved.*

This means that anyone, who wants to, can claim that promise. This verse makes it clear that salvation is available to anyone. Color, national origin, man, woman, young or old, all have the same opportunity.

We need to take a look at another verse at this time.

Mat. 7:21 *Not everyone who says to me, 'Lord, Lord,' shall enter into the kingdom of heaven, but he who does the will of my Father in heaven.*

At first look, it appears that Rom. 10:13 and Mat. 7:21 is a contradiction. Does this mean that there is a list of rules we must follow besides accepting Jesus as our Savior? The answer to that is a resounding NO. There is nothing you can do to save yourself.

If there were, Jesus would not have needed to die on the cross. Let us look at the statement "but he who does the will of the Father" What is the will of the Father?

II Pet. 3:9 *The Lord is not slack concerning His promise, as some count slackness, but is longsuffering toward us, "not willing that any should perish but that all should come to repentance.*

God wants everyone to repent including you, and for you to accept Jesus as your savior.

When you accept Jesus as your Savior you are born again.

1 Pet. 1:23 *Jesus answered and said to him, most assuredly, I say to you, unless one is born again, he cannot see the kingdom of God.*

You become a new creation.

II Cor. 5:17 *Therefore, if anyone is in Christ, he is a new creation: old things have passed away; behold, all things become new.*

The way to salvation is to believe in Jesus Christ and what He did on Calvary's cross. We must believe that Jesus came to earth as a perfect human. He was born of a virgin and walked for 331/2 years without sin. Then shed His blood on the cross to pay the penalty for our sin and sins. He then descended into Hell for three days rose from the dead and spent a short time here on earth before ascending into Heaven to set at the right hand of God. You cannot just believe this as head knowledge, it must be so true to you that it is embedded in your heart.

Before I accepted the Lord as my Savior, I was wild and reckless. Immediately after asking Jesus to come into my heart my old life no longer interested me. I just wanted to live as He wanted me to live. That was when the old things passed away and all things became new. It was as if a huge weight was lifted off my shoulders, and that is exactly what happened. The burden of sin was gone.

The following verses are the biblical proof for this paragraph.

Jesus Christ is the only answer.

Mat. 1:21 *And she will bring forth a Son, and you shall call His name Jesus, for He will save His people from their sin.*

He was without sin. Jesus was the perfect man who paid the penalty for our sins.

1 Peter 2:22 Who committed no sin, nor was deceit found in His mouth.

He was crucified.

Col. 1:21,22 *And you, that were sometime alienated and enemies in your mind by wicked works, yet now hath he reconciled*

22In the body of his flesh through death, to present you holy and unblameable and unreproveable in his sight:

Descended into Hell.

Eph. 4:9 *"He ascended" what does it mean but that He also first descended into the lower parts of the earth?*

He arose from the dead.

1 Cor. 15:4 *and that He was buried, and that He rose again the third day according to the Scriptures.*

Was seen by many.

1 Cor. 15:6 *After that He was seen by over five hundred brethren at once,*

Ascended up to Heaven.

Acts 1:9 *Now when He had spoken these things, while they watched, He was taken up, and a cloud received Him out of their sight.*

Seated at the right hand of God.

Eph. 1:20 *which He worked in Christ when He raised Him from the dead and seated Him at His right hand in the heavenly places.*

You must believe this is who Jesus is and what He did for you. Believe in your heart! This entire process is an act of faith on your part.

Rom. 2:8,9 *For by grace are you saved by faith! and that not of yourselves: it is the gift of God: not of works, lest any man should boast.*

What is faith?

Heb. 11:1 *Now faith is the substance of things hoped for, the evidence of things not seen.*

You are accepting Jesus by faith.

Jn. 20:29 *Jesus said unto him, Thomas, because you have seen me, you have believed: blessed are they who have not seen me and believed.*

You must now tell God that you want to repent of your

sins and accept Jesus as your Lord and Savior. I will give you a prayer to read just after I make this last statement. Saying the words in the following prayer does not save you. It is the belief in your heart, and only that belief, that tells God you are truly repenting of your sins and believe in the blood of Jesus to save your soul. You do not have to be with a preacher or in a church to do this. God will hear you and read your heart even if you are alone.

Dear God in Heaven, I come to you today as a sinner

I am asking you that you save my soul and cleanse me from all sin.

I realize in my heart my need of salvation, which can only come through Jesus Christ.

I am accepting Christ and, what He did on the Cross, into my heart to gain my redemption.

In obedience to your Word, I confess with my mouth the Lord Jesus and believe in my heart that God raised Him from the dead.

You have said in your Word, which cannot lie, for whosoever shall call upon the Name Lord shall be saved.

I have called upon Your Name, in my heart, as You have said, and I believe that right now, I am saved.

Congratulations, you are now Born again. Your soul and spirit have been renewed and you are no longer separated from God. You have full access to God through Jesus Christ and what He did for you on the Cross. Start reading the Bible. You will now have the Holy Spirit who will give you understanding as you read. I would suggest you start in the book of John.

Chapter 9

Benefits of Salvation

You are now a child of God. You were, at the moment you accepted Jesus Christ as your Lord and Savior, and you were baptized into the Body of Christ.

1 Cor. 12:13 *For by one Spirit we were all baptized into one body—whether Jews or Greeks, whether slaves or free—and have all been made to drink into one Spirit.*

1 Cor 12:27 *Now you are the body of Christ, and members individually.*

Each individual Christian makes up the body of Christ, also known as the Church. Not the building, but the body of Christ. Being baptized into the body of Christ is not water baptism, it is the Holy Spirit baptizing you, spiritually, into the Church.

If you are in the body of Christ, what do you have?

1 Jn. 5:11,12 *And this is the record; that God given to us Eternal Life; and this life is in His son. He who has the Son has life; and he who has not the Son of God has not life.*

The first and most important gift you will ever receive is Eternal Life. You also have in Jesus, wisdom, righteousness, sanctification, and redemption.

1 Cor 1:30 *But of Him you are in Christ Jesus, who became*

for us wisdom of God—and righteousness and sanctification and redemption.

He also gives you a comforter and a teacher.

Jn. 14:26 *But the comforter, which is the Holy Spirit, whom the Father will send in My Name, He shall teach you all things, and bring all things to your remembrance, whatsoever I have said unto you.*

How does the Holy Spirit teach you all things? The Holy Spirit will speak to you from the Bible Scriptures. The better you know the Bible the more the Holy Spirit teaches you. The amount of time you spend in the Word of God the more you will grow spiritually. Little time reading and studying the Bible, little growth. A lot of time reading and studying the Bible, much growth.

You also have access to all things the Father has given to Jesus Christ.

Jn. 16:15 *All things the Father has are mine: therefore, said I, that He shall take of mine, and shall show it unto you.*

You can claim all that the Father has given Jesus Christ by accepting what He did on the cross. What Jesus did there is the door to every need you may ever have. All by faith. The Bible is the Word of God, you just have to believe what it says, and, by faith accept it. God will now give you everything you need, not want, but need.

Until this time Satan has controlled you, and, determined your destiny. Since you accepted God's plan for salvation Satan no longer has power over you. He does not like what you have done and will use every means available, to Him, to get you to change your mind. He will plant thoughts in your mind. Examples, you will have thoughts that what you did is not real, such as, You would be better off to go back to the way you were. You must remember, these thoughts are not true. Satan is a deceiver and a liar and will use every trick at his disposal to get you to change your mind.

Jn. 8:44 *You are of your father the devil, and the desires of your father you want to do. He was a murderer from the beginning, and does not stand in the truth, because there is no truth in him. When he speaks a lie, he speaks from his own resources, for he is a liar and the father of it.*

When these thoughts come, go back to the verses we have read in this book. Believe them, not believing them calls God a liar. As we have already determined that the Bible is the word of God, and, God never goes back on His word.

You should now ask God to lead you to a good church, and then attend the services faithfully. Find someone you like being with who is living a Christian life. Leave your old friends. If you continue hanging around them, they will pull you back into the worldly ways.

If you truly seek a church to attend you will find it. The Bible says, if you seek you shall find.

Mat. 7:7 *Ask, and it will begiven to you; seek and you will find; knock, and it will be opened to you.*

You can count on it. That is God's promise to you, and He always keeps His promises.

Some people think that now everything is going to be perfect. Look at Jesus' life. He was constantly ridiculed and scorned and then crucified. Why should things be better for you? You have eternal life now, and as I stated before, Satan will come at you from every angle he can to keep you from being used by God.

The Bible tells us the following.

John 16:33 *These things I have spoken unto you, that in me ye might have peace. In the world ye shall have tribulation: but be of good cheer; I have overcome the world.*

1 Corinthians 10:13 *There hath no temptation taken you but such as is common to man: but God is faithful, who will not suffer you to be tempted above that ye are able; but will with the temptation also make a way to escape, that ye may be able to bear it.*

Remember these verses as they will help you to escape Satan's attacks. This does not mean that you will not be tested and tried, God uses these trials to teach you, instead thank Him for the tribulations you are going through, as He is teaching you what He wants you to know. In His time He will show you, and you will become a better person. Sometimes a verse will jump out of the Bible and into your head as you are reading the Bible, at that time you will know that it is God's answer. Other times your head will be filled with the answer. God is using all of this to conform you into the image of Jesus. You will never be perfect in this lifetime, but when you are raised up into Heaven you will then be perfect.

SECTION THREE

The Guide to Victorious Christian Living

Chapter 10

The New Christian

Now that you are a born-again Christian, what do you do next? When you buy an appliance or any other piece of equipment you receive an instruction booklet or owner's manual. That booklet or owner's manual teaches you how to use the item you just purchased.

The Bible is the owner's manual for your life, and it teaches you how to live a victorious Christian life. The Bible also teaches you that Jesus Christ and Calvary's cross are the answer to any situation you may ever encounter. However, the Bible is a large book and it could take a very long time to find the scriptures that refer to any given circumstance. For this reason, I will list some of the first steps you should take. These steps will help you start living a victorious Christian life.

1. The very first step you need to take is to make God number one in your life. This must be a condition of your heart not just knowledge in your head. The secret of a happy life is giving God the first part of your day, the first priority to every decision, and the first place in your heart.

Mathew 6:33 But seek ye first the kingdom of God, and his righteousness; and all these things shall be added unto you.

Your every thought should be about Him. Everything needs to be about Him. The following verse tells you where God should be in your life. And he answering said,

Mark 10:27 Thou shalt love the Lord thy God with all thy heart, and with all thy soul, and with all thy strength, and with all thy mind; and thy neighbor as thyself.

This verse tells us everything you do should be governed by your love for Him. Every one of your thoughts and actions should be for His glory. That means He comes before your family, your dreams, and before all your possessions. To love the Lord with all your heart, with all your soul, and with all your mind, God needs to be number one in your life.

Two of Jesus' disciples are a good example of making God number one. The Bible says, And Jesus, walking by the Sea of Galilee, saw two brethren, Simon called Peter, and Andrew his brother, casting a net into the sea: for they were fishermen.

Matthew 4:18-20 And He said unto them, follow Me and I will make you fishers of men. And they straightway left their nets and followed Him.

Notice they immediately abandoned their nets, they did not first go home to tell their family, they did not put their nets away, they immediately followed Him. This is the type of commitment God wants from all His followers.

Your eternal destiny has been purchased by the sacrifice Jesus made on the Cross. You now belong to the Lord. You have been bought with a price; you were purchased with the blood of Jesus Christ.

1 Peter 1:18,19 *Inasmuch as ye know that ye were not redeemed with corruptible things, as silver and gold, from your vain conversation received by tradition from your fathers; But with the precious blood of Christ, as of a lamb without blemish and without spot.*

When you accepted Jesus as your Savior you became a new creature. Your soul and spirit are new (born again).

2 Corinthians 5:17 *Therefore, if any man be in Christ, he is a new creature; old things are passed away; behold, all things are become new.*

The Holy Spirit takes up residence in your heart the moment you accept Jesus as your savior.

1 Corinthians 6:19,20*: Do you not know that your body is the temple of the Holy Spirit, which is in you, which you have of God? For you are bought with a price: Therefore, glorify God in your spirit, which are God's.*

I cannot repeat this enough, God must always be number one in your heart.

People often ask, "Why am I here, what does God want from me"? This is the age-old question humanity has been asking. Here is the answer to that question. The Bible tells us you were created to bring glory to God.

Isaiah 43:7 *Even everyone who is called by my name: for I have created him for My glory, I have formed him; yes, I have made him.*

Everything you do should be with the idea of bringing glory to God. This should be your consuming desire.

He wants a close personal relationship with you, when you attain that relationship, He will be able to work His will through you. Putting God first gives the Holy Spirit free reign to conform you to the image of Jesus. In other words, put your faith in what the Bible says Jesus did for you on the cross. Not on anything else. When you consistently do that, The Holy Spirit will teach you all He wants you to know.

2. One of the next things you must do is to separate yourself from those who do not believe in the Lord Jesus Christ and that are not living for Him.

2 Corinthians 6:17 Wherefore come out from among them, and be ye separate, saith the Lord, and touch not the unclean thing; and I will receive you,

2 Thessalonians 3:6 Now we command you, brethren, in the name of our Lord Jesus Christ, that ye withdraw yourselves from every brother that walketh disorderly, and not after the tradition which he received of us.

What are the previous two verses saying? Lets say you have a group of friends that you have been palling around with prior to accepting Jesus. You need to walk away from those friends if they are not following Christ. Then you need to find new friends who are walking in God's will. Why should you do this? Because your old friends are living in the world and enjoying the things of this world. Continuing in that relationship will pull you back to living for the world. You cannot live for God and the world at the same time.

2 Corinthians 6:14 Be not unequally yoked together with

unbelievers: for what fellowship has righteousness with unrighteousness? And, what communication has light with darkness?

This means that you need to separate yourself from them. You do not isolate yourself from them, you remain friendly to them. You do not love what they do or say, but you still love them. you just do not participate in what they do. It is your love for them, and the way you live your life that will draw them to the Lord and allow Him to save their souls from eternal damnation. By doing this your life becomes a witness for Jesus Christ.

3. Next, if you want to grow in the Lord, you must "begin reading the Bible every day." The Word of God is the only true source of wisdom and knowledge.

Proverbs 2:1-6 My son, if you will receive My Words, and hide my commandments with you; so that you incline your ear unto wisdom, and apply your heart to understanding; yes, if you cry after knowledge, and lift up your voice for understanding; if you seek her as silver, and search for her as for hid treasure; Then shall you understand the fear of the Lord and find the knowledge of God. For the Lord gives wisdom: out of His mouth comes knowledge and understanding.

What does it mean, out of His mouth? What comes out of the mouth of the Lord is His Word, and His Word is the Bible. By spending time reading the Bible you will gain wisdom and knowledge directly from the Lord. It is not necessary to read for a long time each day. Try fifteen to twenty minutes a day at first. You may have tried reading the Bible before you accepted the Lord as your Savior, but you could not understand what it was saying.

That is because you did not have the Holy Spirit residing in your heart. Now that you are a child of God, He will begin to open the Word up to your understanding. He will determine what He wants you to learn each time you read. Jesus said,

John 14:26 But the Comforter, which is the Holy Spirit, whom the Father will send in My Name, He shall teach you all things and bring all things to your remembrance, whatsoever I give unto you.

The book of First Peter tells you that as a new Christian, you are just like a newborn baby, and like a baby you need to grow in wisdom and knowledge. When a baby is born it needs milk. Without that milk, it will not grow. It is the same in your Christian life. The Bible tells us,

1 Peter 2:2 *as newborn babes, desire the sincere milk of the word, that you may grow thereby.*

To grow in wisdom and knowledge you must spend time in the Bible. To do this it is necessary to develop a system of Bible reading every day. The Bible is how The Holy Spirit speaks to you and teaches you. Three chapters in the Old Testament and one in the New Testament, each day, will get you through the entire Bible in one year.

What happens when you spend time every day reading and studying the Bible? You read in the book of Psalms,

Psalms 1:1-3 Blessed is the man who walks not in the counsel of the ungodly, nor stands in the way of the sinners, nor sits in the seat of the scornful. But his delight is in the Law of the Lord; and in His law does he meditate day and night. And he shall be like a tree planted by the rivers of water, that brings forth His fruit in His season; his leaf also shall not wither; And whatsoever he does shall prosper.

What a great promise from God. This promise is given to you for just reading and studying the Bible every day. God wants only the very best for you. All He wants from you in return is your love, loyalty, and obedience. How do you show your love to God?

John 14:15 *If ye love me, keep my commandments.*

4. Prayer: God wants more than anything else, to have a very close and personal relationship with you. He wants you to worship, to be in awe of, to praise, to thank, and to make your needs known to Him. You do all of these through prayer. Prayer is not all fancy words; it is just normal communication with God the Father as we would have with anyone else. It is His command to pray without ceasing. Rejoice evermore.

1 Thessalonians 5:16-18 Pray without ceasing. In everything give thanks: for this is the will of God in Christ Jesus concerning you.

Now we know that we cannot be on our knees all the time. The previous scripture refers to a heart attitude of continual worship, praise, and thanksgiving as well as running all our thoughts before Him. Whenever you start to do anything, mention it to your heavenly Father first. This gives the Holy Spirit the opportunity to lead you at all times and in all the things you do. The downside to not running everything before God is that you will make the wrong decisions and be out of His will. There is no peace and joy when you are out of God's will.

When the disciples asked Jesus to teach them to pray Jesus gave the blueprint on how to pray in the form of the Lord's Prayer.

Matthew 6:9-13 Our Father Who is in Heaven, Hallowed be Your Name. Your Kingdom come, Your Will be done in earth, as it is in Heaven. Give us this day our daily bread, and forgive us our debts, as we forgive our debtors. And lead us not into temptation but deliver us from evil: For Yours is the Kingdom, and the power, and the Glory, forever. Amen.

Let's break these verses down.

1. (Our Father who is in Heaven) This tells us to address our prayers to God the Father.

2. (Hallowed be Your Name) Here we recognize the supremacy and holiness of God. We should be in awe of Him for who He is, Holy, Righteous, all-loving, and long-suffering. It tells us to worship Him for who He is. The creator of Heaven and Earth, the great I Am, the all-powerful, and all-knowing God. Our hearts should be overflowing with praise and adoration to God for sending His Son, Jesus Christ, to pay the penalty for our sin and sin's, and giving us the hope of eternal life with Him.

3. (Your Kingdom come; Your will be done in earth as it is in Heaven.) God's will certainly is not the condition you find on earth at present.

   We are also not doing a very good job of spreading the Gospel to every creature as we are instructed in the Great Commission.

Mark 16:15 And he said unto them, go ye into all the world, and preach the gospel to every creature.

The day is coming, the second coming of Christ, that His kingdom will come, and His will, will be done on the earth. This will take place during the millennial reign, the 1000-year reign of Jesus on earth following the 7-year tribulation. During this time Jesus Christ will rule the world in peace and prosperity. There will be no more pain or sorrow. Everything will be in harmonious perfection. However, we can ask Him that during this life to let His will be done and His kingdom come in our hearts and in our actions until His return.

4. Give us this day our daily bread). This is not just talking about the physical nourishment you need, but also for other miscellaneous needs you might have, such as your spiritual needs and for wisdom and knowledge from His Word. You can pray for your family members, friends, and the lost of this world.

During this time, you should not only ask for your needs, but also thank Him for all He has given you. The first thing we need to thank Him for is your salvation. Some other things that are given to all mankind, regardless of their relationship with Jesus Christ, are the air we breathe, the water we drink, the food we eat and the ground we walk on. You need to thank Him for everything you have. We all have numerous items we can thank Him for. With a little thinking, you can find any number of things to thank Him for.

God desires to give us everything that we desire as long as it is in his will. We have all prayed for things that we never received. The following verse tells us why we don't receive some of the things we pray for.

Mark 16:15 Ye lust, and have not: ye kill, and desire to have, and cannot obtain: ye fight and war, yet ye have not, because ye ask not. Ye ask, and receive not, because ye ask amiss, that ye may consume it upon your lusts.

When you ask Him for things, you should make sure and include, if it is your will." He will not give you things that are not in His will for you. Jesus prayed in this manner as you can see in the following verse. And he was withdrawn from them about a stone's cast, and keeled down, and prayed,

Luke 22:42 *Saying, Father, if thou be willing, remove this cup from me: nevertheless not my will, but thine, be done.*

5. (Forgive us our debts as we forgive our debtors.) We now ask forgiveness for our daily sins, including unknown sins.

(1 John 1:9) *If we confess our sins, he is faithful and just to forgive us our sins, and to cleanse us from all unrighteousness.*

God is just waiting for us to ask Him for forgiveness for our sins. God says He will forgive us as we forgive others. Therefore, we must forgive those who hurt us or have done us wrong, even if they do not seek our forgiveness. If we do not forgive others, we cannot expect God to forgive us, and He will not.

Matthew 5:44 *But I say unto you, Love your enemies, bless them that curse you, do good to them that hate you, and pray for them which despitefully use you, and persecute you;*

This does not mean we must have a relationship with them, just do not hold a grudge in your heart. Remember that Jesus forgave us when He went to the Cross and shed His blood. This sacrifice was for every person who ever lived and who will ever live in the future. The Bible states,

Romans 5:8 But God commendeth his love toward us, in that, while we were yet sinners, Christ died for us.

God's love for us is so strong that He sacrificed His only begotten Son to pay the penalty for all of our sins, and for the sins of the entire world. How can we justify not forgiving those who do us wrong? We do not have to love what they do, but we must love them.

6. (And lead us not into temptation but deliver us from evil.) Of course, we do not believe that God would lead us into temptation. Here we are admitting that we are not perfect and need His guidance in resisting temptation and to keep us from the sins we would involve ourselves in. We are simply asking Him to guide us in the footsteps of Jesus. We are also asking Him to protect us from the attacks of Satan and his demons. Jesus defeated Satan on the cross and we need to claim that victory for ourselves.

7. (For Yours is the Kingdom, and the power, and the glory forever.) Here we are confessing that the entire universe belongs to God and that it is controlled by Him, and He deserves all the glory for His creation. We are ending as we started, giving Him praise and worship.

8. (Amen) Remember that we are addressing God the Father, but through Jesus Christ, so before we say amen, we need to say, "I ask this in the name of Jesus Christ." Jesus tells the disciples,

John 16:23 Verily, verily, I say unto you, whatsoever you shall ask the Father in My name, He will give it you.

This verse tells us that we are to address God the Father in the name of, and through Jesus Christ. It does not tell us to address Jesus himself, the Holy Spirit, any dead saint, a priest, or even Mary. Why do we need to ask in Jesus' name? The Bible tells us,

First Timothy 2:5 for there is one God and one mediator between God and men, The Man Christ Jesus.

Jesus Christ is our mediator to God the Father. He pleads our case. This statement can be said at the beginning or at the end of your prayer. It is just a reminder that we have access to God through Jesus Christ our mediator.

5. Church attendance: The Bible tells us we need to attend church so we can worship God with other believers and gain wisdom from His Word for our spiritual growth. The early church devoted themselves to the apostles as a group, for worship, for fellowship, to the breaking of bread, and to prayer.

Acts 2:46,47 And they, continuing daily with one accord in the temple, and breaking bread from house to house, did eat their meat with gladness and singleness of heart,

47Praising God, and having favour with all the people. And the Lord added to the church daily such as should be saved.

Church attendance is not just a "good suggestion"; it is God's will for believers.

Hebrews 10:25 Not forsaking the assembling of ourselves together, as the manner of some is; but exhorting one another: and so much the more, as ye see the day approaching.

Meeting together in church also allows us to build each other up as we all need from time to time.

6. Share what Jesus has done for you. There are numerous

scripture verses that tell us to share our story with others. I will list a few of them. The man, out of whom the devils were expelled, besought him that he might be with him: but Jesus sent him away, saying,

Luke 8:39 *Return to thine own house, and shew how great things God hath done unto thee. And he went his way, and published throughout the whole city how great things Jesus had done unto him.*

Then said Jesus to them again,

(John 20:21) Peace be unto you: as my Father hath sent me, even so send I you.

Another example is,

Acts 3:6-9 *Then Peter said, Silver and gold have I none; but such as I have I give thee: In the name of Jesus Christ of Nazareth rise up and walk. And he took him by the right hand, and lifted him up: and immediately his feet and ankle bones received strength. And he leaping up stood, and walked, and entered with them into the temple, walking, and leaping, and praising God. And all the people saw him walking and praising God:*

The man's walking, jumping, and praising God, in front of all the people, was an act of witnessing.

1 Peter 3:15 But sanctify the Lord God in your hearts: and be ready always to give an answer to every man that asketh you a reason of the hope that is in you with meekness and fear:

This verse tells us to be ready and able to witness at all times.

One of the best ways to witness is to share your testimony. To do this you need to start a conversation with someone. Then in love and meekness get them to share some of their life with you. Be patient, show interest in what they are saying. They want to know you care for them. After a little while, and as opportunity presents itself, you can ask them what their thoughts are about eternal life. Just do not rush it, let time work it out. Somewhere along the way, you may have the opportunity to share your testimony. This all may be a little overwhelming at first, but soon you will be able to do it with confidence. The more Scripture you know the easier this will be.

Pray about witnessing. Ask God to give you boldness and the ability to witness. Remember you have the Holy Spirit to guide you and to teach you. Expect positive things to happen.

Acts 1:8 But ye shall receive power, after that the Holy Ghost is come upon you: and ye shall be witnesses unto me both in Jerusalem, and in all Judaea, and in Samaria, and unto the uttermost part of the earth.

Where we are at any given time is where you need to be a witness. Also, remember that the way you live your life is a testimony.

What have we learned in this chapter?

1. God must become number one in our lives.

2. We must come out from among our old unsaved friends who are living in the world. Separate ourselves from them.

3. We need to establish a Bible reading program for every day.

4. We must develop a daily prayer life.

5. We need to attend church for worship, learning, comfort, and spiritual growth.

6. We need to be ready to give our testimony where and whenever we have an opportunity.

As you put these 6 steps to work in your life the Holy Spirit will bring other areas to mind that He wants to teach you. I list these six just to get you started. They are the building blocks that you can use to develop your victorious Christian life. If you follow them, you will grow in faith and develop a very close daily walk with God your Father. You will find as you do these things God will bless you far more than you ever imagined or deserved. He wants to have a very close relationship with you and to be able to work through you to reach the world. This is how you bring glory to Him.

Chapter 11

Baptism

Christianity immerses us into many new things: A new status, a new identity, a new power. The Bible uses the word Baptism meaning "immersion" to describe these new changes. As you study you will find that there are three separate baptisms found in the Bible.

1. The first baptism is at the time of salvation. At the moment of salvation, the Holy Spirit baptizes you into the body of Christ. The body of Christ is made up of every born-again Christian in the world, also referred to as the church. These born-again Christians are the church. Not the building. Neither is it a denomination.

Galatians 3:26-28 For you are all the children of God by faith in Christ Jesus. For as many of you as have been baptized into Christ have put on Christ. There is neither Jew nor Greek, there is neither bond nor free, there is neither male nor female for you are all one in Christ Jesus

Death, spiritual death, is defeated and you are given eternal life. All nationalities, all ethnicity's, men, and women, are now equal, and all have equal rights to the victories Jesus gained on the Cross. We are now one body in Jesus Christ.

2. The second baptism is water baptism. This baptism is you giving a public declaration to the world that you have accepted Jesus as your savior and that you

are now living your life for Him. You are identifying with the death, burial, and resurrection of Jesus. This is why you need to be immersed. Immersion is a symbolic way of saying that you have been crucified, buried, and have risen with Jesus Christ. You have already been baptized into the Body of Christ and are now placing your total trust in, and total reliance on, the Lord Jesus Christ.

While water baptism is an outward expression of your salvation, it has no part in saving you. It is a testimony to your first baptism, accepting Jesus Christ as your Lord and Savior. An example of this baptism is when Jesus was baptized by John the Baptist.

Matthew 3:13 Then came Jesus from Galilee to Jordan unto John, to be baptized of him.

This verse lets us know that water baptism is not necessary for salvation, it does not wash away sin. Jesus had no sin to be cleansed from, therefore His water baptism was a testimony to the world, not an act of salvation. Remember, we are saved by grace through faith, apart from works.

Ephesians 2:8–9 For by grace are you saved by faith; and that not of yourselves: it is the gift of God: not of works, lest any man should boast.

If salvation required water baptism, that baptism would be a form of works, our own effort. If we could be saved by our own effort there would be no reason for Jesus Christ to have been crucified.

Not only are we baptized as a testimony, we are baptized because our Lord commanded it:

Matthew 28:19 "Go therefore and make disciples of all the nations, baptizing them in the name of the Father and the Son and the Holy Spirit".

Being born again is the only prerequisite to water baptism. The conversion of the Ethiopian Eunuch is a great example of the timing of water baptism coming after salvation.

Acts 8:36-39 And as they went on their way, they came unto a certain water: and the Eunuch said, see, here is water; what does hinder me to be baptized? And Phillip said, if you believe with all your heart, you may. And he answered and said, I believe that Jesus Christ is the Son of God.

The Eunuch first believed and then was baptized in water. The Chief Ruler is another example that salvation comes first, then baptism.

Acts 18:8 And Crispus, the Chief Ruler of the synagogue, believed on the Lord with all his house; and many of the Corinthians hearing believed, and were baptized.

They believed first and then were baptized. If you have not been baptized, since your conversion, seek out your pastor and discuss it with him.

The third baptism is the Baptism of the Holy Spirit, with the evidence of speaking in tongues. This speaking in tongues is the believer's prayer language given to all who have been baptized in the Holy Spirit. Also known as praying in the spirit.

1 Corinthians 1:14 For he that speaketh in an unknown tongue speaketh not unto men, but unto God: for no man understandeth him; howbeit in the spirit he speaketh mysteries.

At the moment of salvation, the Holy Spirit came to

live in your heart. His purpose was to sanctify you. This means He will help you change your ways, from living for the world to walking in the footsteps of Jesus. He will gradually convict you of the things you should no longer do and will reveal the things you should do. This process will continue until the day you make your home in heaven. He empties you of yourself and then fills you with the fruits of the Spirit.

Galatians 5:22,23 *But the fruit of the Spirit is love, joy, peace, longsuffering, gentleness, goodness, faith,*

23Meekness, temperance: against such there is no law.

This process is called sanctification.

When you are baptized with the Holy Spirit, not only is He present in your heart, but you then are immersed in Him. Your whole being is now filled with the Holy Spirit. You may ask yourself, what is the results of being baptized with the Holy Spirit? The following verse gives you an idea of what you get.

Acts 1:8 *But you shall receive power, after that the Holy Spirit is come upon you: and you shall be witnesses unto Me both in Jerusalem, and in all Judea, and in Samaria, and the uttermost part of the earth.*

You shall receive power is the key element in this verse.

When you receive the Baptism if the Holy Spirit you feel closer to the Lord, your prayer life gets stronger and you love to witness to anyone who will listen. You become bold in your witnessing. Even reading the Bible seems to come to life more, and you can discern more.

In Acts chapter three we see Peter and John, under the

power of the Holy Spirit, heal a lame beggar. Many people saw that miracle and were gathering around. Because of what Peter and John were doing and saying, the Sadducee's had them arrested. Now if this happened to most of us, we would be very worried as these were the same people who had just crucified Jesus. They had the power to do the same to Peter and John, or they could have them put in jail or have them stoned. What did Peter do?

Acts 4:8-13 *Then Peter, filled with the Holy Ghost, said unto them, Ye rulers of the people, and elders of Israel, 9 If we this day be examined of the good deed done to the impotent man, by what means he is made whole; 10 Be it known unto you all, and to all the people of Israel, that by the name of Jesus Christ of Nazareth, whom ye crucified, whom God raised from the dead, even by him doth this man stand here before you whole. 11 This is the stone which was set at nought of you builders, which is become the head of the corner. 12 Neither is there salvation in any other: for there is none other name under heaven given among men, whereby we must be saved. 13 Now when they saw the boldness of Peter and John, and perceived that they were unlearned and ignorant men, they marveled; and they took knowledge of them, that they had been with Jesus.*

Peter spoke directly to the Sadducees and the Pharisees. He was not worried about what might happen to him, but instead was very confident about what he was saying. He accused them to their face for all that they had done to Jesus. This is an example of the power and boldness one gets from being filled with the Holy Spirit. You stand with the Lord regardless of the consequences.

There are those who will tell you that you receive all

this at the moment of salvation. You can see that salvation and being filled with the Holy Spirit are two separate experiences from the following verse.

Acts 19:2 He said unto them, Have ye received the Holy Ghost since ye believed? And they said unto him, We have not so much as heard. Whether there be any Holy Ghost.

This was Paul addressing the Galatians. These people were already believers but they received the baptism of the Holy Spirit after salvation. Whether it is 5 minutes or 5 years after you are saved, it makes no difference, there is still a gap between the two acts, it is a separate baptism.

We also find that the baptism of the Holy Spirit was not just meant for the early church but also for the church presently, and in the future.

Acts 2:39 For the promise is unto you, and to your children, and to all who are far off, even as many as the Lord our God shall call.

I have only scratched the surface of this subject. I would recommend that you do a study on it for yourselves. If you do a study proceed with an open mind. If you have an agenda when you begin your study you will find isolated verses to prove your way of thinking. Be honest in your study.

You have now learned that there are three distinct baptisms.

1. Baptized by the Holy Spirit into Christ. (Salvation)
2. Baptized in water. (Declaration)
3. Baptism of the Holy Spirit. (Power)

Use these Baptisms to make you a stronger Evangelist, Preacher Teacher, Church Planter, or in your daily walk with your Lord.

Chapter 12

Principalities and Powers

We read in the Bible that we are in a spiritual battle between the powers of darkness, (Satan), and the Spirit of God. This battle takes place in the spirit world and affects all that we as Christians do.

Whenever the Holy Spirit begins a work in the life of a soul, Satan immediately starts his own campaign to counteract what God has started. Our struggle is defined in this verse.

Eph. 6:10-12 Finally, my brethren, be strong in the Lord, and in the power of His might. Put on the whole armour of God, that you may be able to stand against the wiles of the devil. For we wrestle not against flesh and blood, but against principalities, against powers, against the rulers of the darkness of this world, against spiritual wickedness in high places. Eph. 6:10-12)

This is the spiritual battle we are in as Christians. We are warned to be aware and vigilant about this war.

1 Peter 5:8 *Be sober, be vigilant; because your adversary the devil, as a roaring lion, walketh about, seeking whom he may devour:*

Satan is constantly looking for our weaknesses so he can attack our faith. This spiritual battle, that we are in, takes place in our mind as you can see in the following verses.

2 Corinthians 10:3-5 For though we walk in the flesh, we do not war after the flesh: For the weapons of our warfare are not carnal, but mighty through God to the pulling down of strong holds; Casting down imaginations, and every high thing that exalteth itself against the knowledge of God, and bringing into captivity every thought to the obedience of Christ;

Satan uses our imagination and thoughts in an effort to dilute and confuse our understanding of God's Word or to doubt it altogether. He wants to steal us from God. He will use our worldly desires and the lusts of our flesh to accomplish this. We must ever be aware of his efforts.
The Bible and prayer are our only defense.

A good example of this spiritual battle is found in the book of Job.

Job 1:10-12 And the LORD said unto Satan, Whence comest thou? Then Satan answered the LORD, and said, from going to and fro in the earth, and from walking up and down in it. And the LORD said unto Satan, Hast thou considered my servant Job, that there is none like him in the earth, a perfect and an upright man, one that feareth God, and escheweth evil Then Satan answered the LORD, and said, Doth Job fear God for nought? Hast not thou made an hedge about him, and about his house, and about all that he hath on every side? thou hast blessed the work of his hands, and his substance is increased in the land. But put forth thine hand now, and touch all that he hath, and he will curse thee to thy face. And the LORD said unto Satan, Behold, all that he hath is in thy power; only upon himself put not forth thine hand. So, Satan went forth from the presence of the LORD.

This was Satan getting permission from God to afflict Job. Satan is always limited as to how far he can go in tempting us. But be aware, he never stops in his attempt to sway us in our belief.

From time to time God allows Satan to try us as you just saw in Job's case. God uses these trials as a method of teaching and faith-building; however, God will limit the severity of those trials, so welcome them as lessons to be learned.

1 Cor. 10:13 *There hath no temptation taken you but such as is common to man: but God is faithful, who will not suffer you to be tempted above that ye are able; but will with the temptation also make a way to escape, that ye may be able to bear it.*

James 1:2,3 *My brethren, count it all joy when ye fall into divers' temptations; Knowing this, that the trying of your faith worketh patience. But let patience have her perfect work, that ye may be perfect and entire, wanting nothing.*

Hebrews 12:5-8 *And ye have forgotten the exhortation which speaketh unto you as unto children, My son, despise not thou the chastening of the Lord, nor faint when thou art rebuked of him:6 For whom the Lord loveth he chasteneth, and scourgeth every son whom he receiveth.7 If ye endure chastening, God dealeth with you as with sons; for what son is he whom the father chasteneth not?8 But if ye be without chastisement, whereof all are partakers, then are ye bastards, and not sons.*

If you can get these three verses down, in your life, you will have made living your Christian life much easier.

So how do we fight this spiritual battle? First, we need to remember that when Jesus gave His life on the Cross, He defeated Satan.

Heb. 2:14 *Forasmuch then as the children are partakers of*

flesh and blood, He also Himself likewise took part of the same; that through death He might destroy him that had the power of death, that is, the devil;

At this point Satan has been completely defeated. He cannot tempt us without God's approval, and God will only allow what is necessary for us to learn and grow by.

God blesses us when we endure His testing.

James 1:12 Blessed is the man that endureth temptation: for when he is tried, he shall receive the crown of life, which the Lord hath promised to them that love him

This verse should be enough to get you through any trials you may encounter. Refer back to the verse 1 Cor. 10:13. You just need to remember that God knows what you are going through, and will not allow you to be tempted beyond what you can endure. Everything God does is perfect. He knows what we need. He shapes us by doing whatever it takes for to us grow. Remember in those times of trials He will not allow us to be tried beyond what we are able to stand, and in the end, we will be the better for those trials.

When we accept Jesus as our Lord and Savior, we have access to the victory Christ won on the Cross. With the shedding of His blood Jesus defeated Satan, and God the Father gave Him access to all things He has in Heaven;

John 16:15 All things that the Father has are mine: therefore, said I, that He shall take of mine, and shall show it unto you.

The word of God lets us know what the victory Jesus won on the Cross accomplished. We then claim that victory for ourselves through prayer. If you try to overcome them on your own you will fail.

To claim victory over Satan the Bible gives us some scriptures to follow.

Eph. 6:14-18 Stand therefore, having your loins gird about with Truth, and the breastplate of righteousness; And your feet shod with the preparation of the Gospel of peace; Above all, taking the Shield of Faith, wherewith you shall be able to quench all the fiery darts of the wicked. And take the Helmet of Salvation, and the Sword of the Spirit, which is in the Word of God; Praying always with all prayer and supplication in the Spirit, and watching thereunto with all perseverance and supplication for all Saints;

How do we acquire these protections? There are two sources of power in the previous scripture. The Word of God and prayer. I cannot say this enough, you must read and study the bible every day so you know the truth when Satan tempts you. Even Jesus used the Word of God to fight the temptations of Satan. And when the tempter came to Him, he said,

I Matthew. 4:3,4 *If You be the Son of God, command that these stones be made bread. But He answered and said, it is written, Man shall not live by bread alone, but by every word that proceeds from the mouth of God.*

If Jesus found it necessary to use the Word when He was tempted by Satan, who are we to do otherwise? You must also spend time in prayer every day claiming this victory. Prayer is one of our strongest defenses against temptation.

What have we learned in this chapter?

1. We are in a war with Principalities and Powers. A spiritual battle that takes place in our mind.

2. This spiritual battle is a means to strengthen our walk with Jesus.

3. We can have victory in this war through Bible study, and prayer, and accepting what Jesus did on the cross for us.

Only Jesus and what He did on the Cross can give us victory. God never lies. Just ask, believe, then receive.

Chapter 13
Fruit of the Spirit

The fruit of the Spirit is a part of God's personality that He wants to impart into our personality. This process is called sanctification. Sanctification is the Holy Spirits work of molding, shaping, and transforming us into the image of Jesus Christ. Sanctification will continue for our entire lifetime.

Philippians 1:6 *Being confident of this very thing, that he which hath begun a good work in you will perform it until the day of Jesus Christ:*

Even though we will not attain perfection in this lifetime, that should be our greatest desire and goal. The Holy Spirit will not force God's personality on us, we must surrender ourselves to His guidance continually and yield ourselves to the leading of the Holy Spirit in order to attain them.

The following verses tells us what the fruits are. But the fruit of the:

Galatians 5:22,23 *Spirit is love, joy, peace, longsuffering (patience), gentleness, goodness, faith, meekness, temperance (self-control): against such there is no law.*

These fruits are one of the many characteristics of God, and He wants to transfer them to His children. How wonderful that God wants us to be like Him.

Let's take a look at these individual attributes and see

where we stand. These are Gods attributes, coming from God to you, and not from the world.

The following statements on the 9 fruits of the Spirit are copied in part from the internet at <www//bibleknowledge.com/fruits-of-the-holy-spirit>. Article by Michael Brady, updated November 19, 2018.

Love:

Here are some of the different definitions on what love is from the different Bible Dictionaries and Commentaries:

- Unselfish, benevolent concern for another; brotherly concern; the object of brotherly concern or affection

- The self-denying, self-sacrificing, Christ-like love which is the foundation of all other graces

- Unselfish, loyal and benevolent concern for the well-being of another

- The high esteem which God has for His human children and the high regard which they, in turn, should have for Him and other people

- To love, to have affection for someone; to like; to be a friend; the love of brothers for each other.

One of the main messages that comes through loud and clear, from studying our Bible, is the extreme importance that God the Father is placing on them, and that everyone learn how to love Him, love one another, and to even go as far as to be able to love our enemies and those who will try and hurt us.

However, our abilities, as fallen humans, to love one

another is very limited.

This is why it is so important for each and every Christian to work very closely with the Holy Spirit to get this fruit worked up into the core of our personalities.

It is only when the love of the Holy Spirit starts to flow and enter into our personalities can we even begin to love God, and love one another to the degree and to the intensity that God would like to see from each one of us.

To those of you entering into this sanctification process with the Lord – this quality should be listed as the #1 quality you should put into the core of your soul and personality.

The Holy Spirit will be moving in you very quickly to grow the quality of love in your heart due to its importance in your walk with Him.

You can be the greatest man of God and have some of the greatest gifts of God flowing through you – but if you are not walking with all of this in the spirit of love and humility, it will have all been for naught.

This is the characteristic that must overshadow all the other gifts.

The Bible tells us,

1 Corinthians 13:2 Though I have the gift of prophecy, and understand all mysteries, and have all knowledge, and though I have all faith, so that I could remove mountains, and have not charity (love), I am nothing.

You may be asking yourself; how do I know I love the Lord? Is it a feeling or what? The following verse makes it very clear.

John 14:15 *If ye love me, keep my commandments.*

Joy: In the rough and tough world, we live in with all of the crime, disorder, and bad things that can happen to any of us at any time, many have lost some of their joy as a result of the beatings they have taken in this life. Through all of this God is waiting to fill you with His joy.

Romans 15:13 *Now the God of hope fill you with all joy and peace in believing, that ye may abound in hope, through the power of the Holy Ghost.*

From the day you accepted Jesus, God has desired to fill you with this joy.

I remember I had a bank teller tell me one time that she very seldom sees people smiling anymore when they come into the bank. She says no one seems to be happy anymore and everyone seems to be carrying around the weight of the world on their shoulders.

Again, with the imperfections of our fallen nature, and then you combine that with how people react differently to adversity – some Christians have had most, if not all of their joy in the Lord, knocked right out of them.

This is why the above verse, Galatians 5:22,23 is so powerful and so needed by every single Christian today. In these verses, God is telling us that He can transmit some of His godly and divine qualities right up into the middle of us. Many of God's people need a fresh infusion of His divine qualities due to the leaks that have occurred as a result of some of the beatings His people have taken during the course of their lives. And the quality of joy is a much-needed quality in this day and age. No matter how bad of a beating you may have taken in this life – God can still fully heal, deliver, and restore you if you are willing to work with Him in this healing process. And one of the things that God can fully restore in you is your joy. And not only can the Lord fully restore what joy you used to have, but He can also increase it to a much greater degree and intensity!

Here are some of the different definitions of what real joy is all about:

1 Great delight; gladness of heart

2 The happy state that results from knowing and serving God

3 That deep, abiding, inner rejoicing in the Lord

4 To rejoice, to be glad

5 Happy, joyful, cheerful, rejoicing, festive

The Bible says that the joy of the Lord is your strength.

Nehemiah 8:10 *Then he said unto them, Go your way, eat the fat, and drink the sweet, and send portions unto them for whom nothing is prepared: for this day is holy unto our Lord: neither be ye sorry; for the joy of the LORD is your strength.*

This is why it is so important that every Christian has some level of God's joy operating through them in this life. Without God's joy operating in your life, things can begin to dry up. Nothing is ever fun anymore. Everything can start to become a chore. Before you know it, you will want to start withdrawing from others and life in general.

The joy of the Lord can really give you an incredible surge of strength in your own daily walk with God – especially when you have to take on some really tough situations.

This is why each Christian should work very closely with the Holy Spirit in not only getting Him to release His joy into their system, but to also keep it running through them on a very regular and consistent basis.

The Holy Spirit will do this for you if you are open to receiving this divine infusion from Him and are willing to work with Him to keep it properly flowing through you on a regular basis.

Peace: This is another major quality that we all need operating in our lives, especially with all the uncertainty of this life and never knowing what is going to happen next.

Jobs are no longer as secure as they used to be. You never know when the company you work for may be bought out and your job will be gone in a flash. Half of all marriages still end in divorce. We are all forced to constantly live under the threat of future terrorist activity, never knowing when or where the next attack will come from.

With all this kind of heightened activity that we are all forced to deal with daily, it becomes very easy to lose your sense of peace, especially your peace in the Lord.

John 14:27 *Peace I leave with you, my peace I give unto you: not as the world giveth, give I unto you. Let not your heart be troubled, neither let it be afraid.*

Again, this is one of the 9 fruits of the Holy Spirit, and the Holy Spirit can really help you pick up the slack if you start losing your own sense of peace over some of the storm clouds that could come against you in this life. The following are three items that will let you know that you are getting Gods peace..

1. The presence and experience of the right relationships
2. The tranquility of the soul

3. Sense of well-being and fulfillment that comes from God and is dependent on His presence

The inner tranquility and poise of the Christian whose trust is in Him, have found that once His peace starts to flow up into your mind, soul, and emotions, it is as the Bible says – a peace that surpasses all human understanding – especially when that peace comes in right in the middle of a severe storm cloud that you may be going through.

Like joy, this peace is from the Lord and grows as you grow in grace. This is perfect peace that helps you through all your trials. When you have this peace, you will be able to endure any trials or tests.

Long-suffering: (patience) One of the main definitions of the word long suffering is that it is referring to patience. And patience is another sorely needed quality in the fast-paced world in which we live today.

2 Peter 3:9 *The Lord is not slack concerning his promise, as some men count slackness; but is longsuffering to us-ward, not willing that any should perish, but that all should come to repentance.*

Just watch people standing in line at the grocery store or at your local fast-food restaurant and watch how short some people's fuses are today. Road rage is still a major problem on some of our highways. Look at someone the wrong way and they will want to try and take your head off. Many people have been killed or seriously injured because someone lost his temper over something very trivial. With the fast-paced ways of our society, many people have had their fuses shortened up and it thus takes very little to set them off. As a result, many people have very little patience operating in their personalities today.

For Christians, this poses a major dilemma. One of the ways of our God is that He is a very patient and long-suffering God. His ways are not our ways.

And one of the things you will find out very early on about His ways is that He works in a much slower time frame than we do. And unless you learn to adjust to His slower way of working things out, you will find yourself easily losing your patience with Him and how He wants to work things out in your life.

You will have to work with the Holy Spirit on this particular quality to get it properly worked up into your personality.

The reason for this is that your own impatience will start to act up and try to override the patience and longsuffering that the Holy Spirit will try and transmit to you. At times, it may become a battle of wills – your will against His will.

But once the Holy Spirit starts to manifest this quality into your personality, you must try and move with it and allow it to get worked into your mind and emotions. If you do this, then His patience will start to override your impatience, and before you know it, your fuses will begin to lengthen and you will not lose your patience like you used to.

Here are the different definitions for the word longsuffering:

1. Forbearance, patience
2. Patient endurance and steadfastness under provocation
3. Forbearance under ill-will, with no thought of retaliation
4. Patience, endurance, steadfastness, and forbearance
5. Forbearance under suffering and endurance in the face of adversity

6. Ability to endure persecution and ill-treatment

With the way all these definitions are reading, you can really see why we all need the patience and longsuffering of the Holy Spirit to start operating in our souls and personalities – especially when we are forced to face any kind of adversity. Sometimes it will be the patience and longsuffering of the Holy Spirit that will be the only thing that will give you the ability to last the entire length of a bad trial.

Learn how to ride and flow with the patience of the Holy Spirit in your daily life and walk with the Lord – and you will then be able to enter a much more restful, peaceful state within your mind and emotions.

Psalms 27:14 Wait on the Lord: be of good courage, and He shall strengthen your heart: wait, I say, on the Lord. ()

Gentleness: (kindness) As a result of more people being impatient, having short fuses, and with everyone always being in a hurry – many people have lost the ability to treat others with kindness and respect. A kind word, a kind action to another person can do wonders for them.

When we study the life of Jesus in the New Testament, we can tell how kind He always was with other people.

Matthew 23:37 *O Jerusalem, Jerusalem, you who kill the prophets, and stone them which are sent unto you, how often would I have gathered your children together, even as a hen gathers her chickens under her wings, and you would not!*

Jesus is without question, the ultimate role model for all of us, of someone who was fully walking and operating in all 9 fruits of the Holy Spirit.

The quality of kindness will go hand in hand with the

quality of love. Once the Holy Spirit starts to transmit His love up into you, the quality of kindness will follow right along with it. It will then become much easier for you to be able to be kind to others once the love of God starts to flow more into your personality.

Here are some of the different definitions of what real kindness is all about:

1. Quality or state of being kind

2. The steadfast love that maintains relationships through gracious aid in times of need

3. Goodness of heart, serviceable, good, gracious, pleasant

4. Love for mankind, hospitality, acts of kindness, readiness to help, human friendship, benevolence, taking thought of others.

5. Goodness in action, sweetness of disposition, gentleness in dealing with others, affability

6. The ability to act for the welfare of those taxing your patience

As you can see from some of these different definitions, this is a very beautiful quality to have transmitted up into your soul and personality by the Holy Spirit. Not only will you be able to touch others with this godly quality, but you will also be able to touch yourself – because you will feel so much better about yourself if you can learn how to treat others with more kindness and respect in your daily dealings and affairs with them.

Goodness: Psalms 31:19 *OH, how great is Your goodness, which You have laid up for them who fear You; which You*

have wrought for them who trust in you before the sons of men;

This quality has a real drawing power to it. Not only does the goodness of God draw people directly to Him, but this fruit of goodness operating in a believer can also draw people directly to God through the actual believer. Spirit-filled saints who are walking with many of these fruits operating through them are like a magnet.

Many people who have been saved through an individual believer say that what drew them in was the love and goodness they saw shining through that believer.

However, there is something extra special about the quality of goodness. Many Christians can effectively witness to others by just living right and being a good example and role model for others to follow. Many nonbelievers carefully watch and study some Christians because they know there is something different about them. One of the key qualities a nonbeliever will pick up on, in a solid Christian, is this quality of goodness. This quality can get down deep into the core of a believer's personality.

This quality is not something that wavers. These people are good down to the very core of their personalities. You can see it and feel it when you get around these types of people.

As a result of seeing this God-like goodness deeply ingrained into their personalities, there is an immediate drawing towards them. You feel totally safe being around them because you know you can totally trust them, and you know they would never deliberately hurt you.

Children are quick to sense and pick up on this quality in people who have it. These types of Christians draw children and adults to them like magnets.

This is why this fruit and quality is so important for each Christian to have. Because with it, you can easily draw many more people to the Lord. The goodness of God will lead people to repentance and salvation, you can have the actual goodness of God shining through you to reach others if you are willing to work with the Holy Spirit in this sanctification process.

Now here are some of the different definitions of what this quality is all about:

1. Beneficence, ready to do good, love in action

2. Kindness in actual manifestation, virtue equipped for action, a bountiful propensity both to will and to do what is good, intrinsic goodness producing a generosity and a Godlike state or being

3. The word beneficence means the fact or quality of being kind or doing good

This quality is a very powerful fruit to have operating in your personality because of the drawing power it has in it. And the beautiful part about this fruit is that this quality is so pure in its goodness – it does not have any manipulative qualities within it.

In other words, a truly good person could not even begin to try and use you or manipulate you for their gain because they are too good and righteous to even begin to think along those lines.

This is God's goodness that the Holy Spirit is building in you, through the process of sanctification. Your life becomes a witness and draws others to the Lord Jesus Christ. This goodness is for the benefit of others and not for your gratification.

Faith: (faithfulness) In the times we live in with half of all marriages still ending up in divorce, and with many people getting backstabbed in the workplaces with people they thought they could initially trust. This quality is one that is really needed in our day and age. This quality is not only needed in our own personal relationship with God, but it is also needed in our relationships with our friends and our families.

Once you are saved and have entered a true personal relationship with the Lord one of the first things you will have to grab a hold of is holding fast to the Lord and staying faithful to Him for the rest of your eternal life.

This is what got the Jewish people in major trouble with God the Father back in the Old Testament. They could not stay faithful and loyal to Him on a consistent and regular basis. There were times when God the Father was calling them harlots and adulterers because they would not stay faithful to Him.

God the Father holds this quality in high esteem, and this is one quality that He will expect you to operate very strongly in. Not only in your own personal relationship with Him, but also in your other personal relationships with your family and friends. In other words, He wants you to be faithful and loyal to Him first, then your spouses, to your children, to your parents, and to your good friends.

Too many people are bailing out from their spouses and their children if they hit a few minor speed bumps in their marriages.

Too many spouses are having affairs behind the other's back, thereby destroying all of the trust and faithfulness that may have been built up in the early years of their marriages.

Too many fathers are bailing out of their marriages, and then forgetting and forsaking their children. Sometimes for good, never wanting to see any of them ever again!

If God brings you a wonderful mate, wonderful children, and good and wonderful friends, He will then expect you to stay loyal and faithful to all of them. A true friend will stay by your side for life – through thick and thin and for better or for worse. Just as God will stay faithful to you in His own personal relationship with you, He will expect you to stay loyal and faithful in your own personal relationships with the other people in your life.

Now here is what some of the different Bible Dictionaries and Commentaries have to say about this particular quality:

1. Fidelity which makes one true to his promise and faithful to his task

2. Steadfast, dedicated, dependable, and worthy of trust

3. Steadfast, unchanging, and thoroughly grounded in relation to the other

4. Dependability, loyalty, and stability

With the self-centered and materialistic world in which we now live, where many people's only goals and ambitions are to get as much as they can out of this life while they still can, I am afraid this is one quality that is in very short supply.

Most people are lucky if they manage to make 2 or 3 good, loyal, and faithful friends in this lifetime.

This is one quality that God the Father is watching all of us on. He is watching who is going to stay true, loyal, and faithful to Him, and who will stay true, loyal, and faithful to the friends and family that are brought into our lives.

The flesh is strong, especially in wanting to satisfy its lust for the material things of this life. This is why this quality is one of the 9 fruits of the Holy Spirit.

We all need the faithfulness of the Holy Spirit worked into us to help us keep loyal to God, family, and friends.

Meekness: Many men may draw back a bit from this next fruit, which is the quality of meekness. Since Jesus walked our earth as a man, the Son of Man, study His actions very carefully when you read the gospels and how He handled different types of people. There were times that He would engage and set people straight, like He did with some of the Scribes and Pharisees. But there were other times that He dealt with people very gently, with kindness and love. His gentle way of handling some of these people is what jumps out at you when you study how He handled different types of people. Again, Jesus is the perfect role model for all of us to study and learn from, especially with how He handled people while He was walking down here on earth. For men in particular, His actions and behavior towards others should be a major study for us and we should seek to pattern our daily walk after Him. And one of the divine qualities that He had operating in Him with great abundance was the quality of meekness.

The quality of meekness is a quality needed in our world today. So many people have been beat up and hurt in their dealings with other people that just a gentle word, a gentle touch from another Christian can really open the door for that person to be able to receive Jesus and His healing, saving, and deliverance power into their lives.

Once you start walking in the Holy Spirit with His divine fruits operating and flowing through you, you will be able to feel and sense when you should handle a certain person or a certain type of situation with more of a touch of meekness rather than with any kind of stern rebuke or condemnation. There is a time for tough love, but there are also times that just a gentle and loving touch is all that is really needed to properly handle a certain situation.

The Holy Spirit will guide you in all of this. Just realize that the quality of meekness is one of the 9 fruits of the Spirit, and this is one of the fruits that He would like to get worked into your personality, especially in being able to use it when dealing with and helping others.

Parents especially need this fruit operating through them, as it is very easy to get out of balance with the way you are correcting your children. Sometimes more of a tough love approach is needed, but at other times more of a gentle approach will be better suited for the situation.

If all your children ever hear from you are stern words of rebuke and criticism, and it is never properly balanced out with words and actions of love, kindness, and meekness then after a certain period of time your children will start to pull away from you, and they then will have no more desire to want to establish any type of good, solid, loving relationship with you.

Now here are some of the different definitions of the quality of gentleness:

1. Mildness combined with tenderness

2. Gracious, kindly disposition, controlled strength

3. A disposition that is even-tempered, tranquil, balanced

in spirit, unpretentious and that has passions under control

4. A character that is equitable, reasonable, forbearing, moderate, fair, and considerate

5. Power and strength under control

6. Willing to pardon injuries, and correct faults. One who rules his spirit well

Not only will other people love and gravitate towards you more if you learn how to walk in this quality but you will be more at peace with yourself since you will not always have to be fighting and striving with others when trying to help them out.

Self-control: This is the ability to control our worldly impulses and lusts.

Proverbs 16:32 He who is slow to anger (self-control) is better than the mighty; and he who rules his spirit than he who takes a city.

Last of the fruits listed, but certainly not least, is the quality of self-control. This one is huge, and I mean huge!

Once you start to enter into a true sanctification process with the Lord expect the Holy Spirit to move on you very early with this specific quality.

The reason for this is that we all have a certain amount of character flaws operating in our personalities. There are some bad and negative qualities that will have to go.

The Bible tells us that our spirits and our flesh will war against each other in this life. Our flesh wants immediate self-gratification at all costs and will stop at nothing to try and get it.

107

Our spirits know that some of our fleshly desires are not right for us and as a result, there will be a tug of war between the two – and sometimes it will be a major tug of war. The only thing that will be able to control and curb some of the desires of our flesh is the quality of self-control.

Since we all live in a very self-centered and materialistic type world today, many people have very poor impulse control. If they see something they immediately want, they will do anything they can to get it. They will not be denied until they get what they are going after. These people are very weak in the quality of self-control.

This is why the Bible tells us that if we can learn how to walk in the Holy Spirit, then we will not fulfill the lusts of our flesh.

Due to our fallen and sinful natures, all of us are weak to some degree in the quality of self-control. This is why God the Father made sure to have this fruit listed as one of the 9 fruits of His Holy Spirit.

We all need God's self-control operating in our lives and in our personalities if we are going to have any hope of getting cleaned up and properly sanctified to the degree that He would like to get us to in this life.

If you do not have God's self-control operating through you, you will have very little victory over such things as bad tempers, and judgmental and critical spirits.

Once the Holy Spirit starts this sanctification process within you be prepared for some major battles and tugs of wars with Him. But if you are willing to yield to Him and allow Him to start to work all 9 of these fruits into your personality, then you will find yourself starting to grow in ways and in areas that you never thought were possible in this life.

His supernatural power in this area will blow you away once you see how far He can take you to become the person that He would like you to become in this lifetime.

Here are some of the definitions of what the quality of self-control is all about:

1. Temperance, rational restraint of natural impulses

2. Sober, temperate, calm, and dispassionate approach to life, having mastered personal desires and passions

3. Calls for a self-disciplined life following Christ's example of being in the world but not of the world

4. Restraint or discipline exercised over one's behavior

The above definitions perfectly describe what God is looking for once He starts to work and transmit this quality into our personalities. This specific quality is one of the major keys in being able to get any kind of victory over some of the lusts and desires of our flesh.

All the attributes of the Fruit of The Spirit are necessary for a successful walk with God. Over time, as you keep them in mind, you will find that the Holy Spirit has made progress in your spiritual maturity. And you will be closer to walking in the footsteps of Jesus.

What have we learned in this chapter?

a. God loves us so much, and that He wants to develop within us His characteristics.

b. We must work with the Holy Spirit, by reading the Bible and being in prayer every day.

c. That the Holy Spirit will continue this process until the day Jesus calls us up to take our place with Him.

This is a lifetime process. It must ever be on your mind. The more we absorb the fruit of the Spirit the better God will be able to use us in His efforts to reach the world with the Gospel.

John 14:27 Peace I leave with you, my peace I give unto you: not as the world gives, give I unto you. Let not your heart be troubled, neither let it be afraid.

Chapter 14

Tithing

Tithing is one of the most important aspects of the victorious Christian's life. Putting God first in our finances prioritizes and blesses our lives.

The paying of tithes was first mentioned in the Old Testament with Abraham paying tithes of the spoils from the conquest of Chedorlaomer, to Melchizedek. Melchizedek praised God for Abraham's victory and said'

Genesis 14:20 And blessed be the Most High God, who has delivered your enemies into your hand. And he (Abraham) gave him tithes of all.

Also, the Bible tells us that tithes are not only mandated for the Jewish people, but they are holy unto the Lord.

Leviticus 27:30 And all the tithe of the land, whether of the seed of the land, or of the fruit of the tree, is the Lord's: it is holy unto the Lord.

Levitical law, which God gave to the people of Israel, through Moses, spoke of a ten percent tithe to the Priesthood.

Numbers 18:21 And, behold, I have given the children of Levi all the tenth in Israel for an inheritance, for their service which they serve, even the service of the Tabernacle of the congregation.

In other words, a tenth was to be given to the church. This was, and still is, God's way to pay for the upkeep of the tabernacle (the church), and to pay the priests (pastors). In those days tithing was the law. People had no choice in their giving. They were required to tithe.

God promises an abundant blessing to those who do tithe.

Malachi 3:10 Bring you all the tithes into the storehouse, that there may be meat in My house, and prove Me now herewith, says the Lord of Hosts, if I will not open you the windows of Heaven, and pour you out a blessing, that there shall not be room enough to receive it.

In this verse God challenges us to test Him with our giving. This is the only place in the Bible where God allows us to test Him. I challenge each one of you to take this challenge. You will love the outcome. You cannot outgive God.

What was God's attitude towards those who did not pay their tithes? He promises a curse on them.

Malachi 3:8,9 Will a man rob God? Yet you have robbed Me. But you say, wherein have we robbed you? In tithes and offerings. You are cursed with a curse: for you have robbed Me, even this whole nation.

In these verses we find that Malachi refers to those who do not pay their tithes as robbers, robbers of God. He promises a curse on them. Whenever God warns us that we are not following His commandments, He always provides a blessing if we will humble ourselves, repent, and turn back to Him and His ways. You can see His promise in this situation in Malachi 3:10 mentioned above.

We have looked at the Old Testament concerning tithing. What about the New Testament teaching? In the Old Testament we learned that God set 10% as the amount needed to sustain the Tabernacle (church) and to sustain the priesthood (pastors).

Why would we expect it to be any less today? The 10% is to be carried over into the church age.

Jesus endorsed tithing when He faulted the Pharisees on their failing to give as much importance to the more important matters of the law.

Matthew 23:23 Woe unto you, scribes and Pharisees, hypocrites! for ye pay tithe of mint and anise and cumin, and have omitted the weightier matters of the law, judgment, mercy, and faith: these ought ye to have done, and not to leave the other undone.

Look at the last part of the last sentence. He tells them that they should do the more important things and also tithe.

Giving is also spoken of in the New Testament, also known to many as offerings.

11 Cor. 9:7 Every man according as he purposeth in his heart, so let him give; not grudgingly, or of necessity: for God loveth a cheerful giver.

This was when Paul was collecting a special offering for the needy in Jerusalem who were being kicked out of their home and jobs because they became Christians. Giving is how we support our missionaries, widows, and the poor. Offerings are just as important as tithing. When we have accepted Jesus as our Savior and have made God number one in our lives, tithes and offerings are something we want to do. It just goes along with what Jesus has done for us.

If I have heard it once I have heard it 1000 times, I cannot even pay my debts let alone give tithes and offerings. You have just arrived at one of the most crucial times in your Christian Walk. Either you are going to accept what the Bible teaches or not, it is up to you. See what God has to say about it in the verses below.

Mathew 6:25-34 Therefore, I say unto you, take no thought for your life, what ye shall eat, or what ye shall drink; nor yet for your body, what ye shall put on. Is not the life more than meat, and the body than raiment?

Behold the fowls of the air: for they sow not, neither do they reap, nor gather into barns; yet your heavenly Father feedeth them. Are ye not much better than they?

Which of you by taking thought can add one cubit unto his stature?

And why take ye thought for raiment? Consider the lilies of the field, how they grow; they toil not, neither do they spin:

And yet I say unto you, that even Solomon in all his glory was not arrayed like one of these.

Wherefore, if God so clothe the grass of the field, which today is, and tomorrow is cast into the oven, shall he not much more clothe you, O ye of little faith?

Therefore, take no thought, saying, what shall we eat? or, what shall we drink? or, Wherewithal shall we be clothed?

(For after all these things do the Gentiles seek:) for your heavenly Father knoweth that ye have need of all these things.

But seek ye first the kingdom of God, and his righteousness; and all these things shall be added unto you.

Take therefore no thought for the morrow: for the morrow shall take thought for the things of itself. Sufficient unto the day is the evil thereof.

God has a unique way of working things out. I guess a good way to explain God's methods for making it possible for you to pay your tithes and offerings would be to tell my own experience. My wife had a series of strokes that left her completely helpless. I became her 24/7 caretaker for the next three and a half years. At the time this first happened, I had two car payments. Three or four credit card payments and a medical payment, along with the normal household bills. We never had dollars left over. We had been tithing but it was less than 10%. The Lord began to work on me about making Him number one in my life and I made the commitment to tithe. I immediately changed my tithe to 10%, however, my income would not cover everything and I would have to put some of my purchases on the credit card. I could have cut my tithe amount but that just did not feel right.

As I prayed about this situation and God began to show me how to cut some of my expenses. I then used that money to apply to the other bills. In about a year and a half, I was debt-free and had money left over at the end of the month. How does He do this, I'm not sure, but He finds a way. I began giving offerings to missionaries in addition to my tithe and at the end of three and a half years, when my wife passed, I had nearly as much in savings as I had in debt at the beginning. God promised to bless us if we followed His commandments, and He did. I cannot say how He will help you but He will.

You must decide if you are going to handle God's money responsibly or waste it. God promises to meet our needs, not our wants. If you will trust Him and allow Him to guide you in your purchases, you will find that things will begin to get better, and you will have money left at the end of the month. Even after you have paid your tithes and offerings.

What have we learned in this chapter?

1. Pay your 10% tithe to your church first, the place where you are being spiritually fed.

2. Give offerings to missionaries, and to those who are in need.

3. Handle your money responsibly.

4. Enjoy all the blessings God has for you.

God expects each one of his children to share in the cost of the church, the pastor, missions, and to those who are in need. Let us all do our part and bring the good news of Jesus Christ to every ear.

Chapter 15

Future Growth

In the first five chapters, I have given you ten topics that will help you to grow in your Christian Walk. If you have taken these topics to heart, it is a good probability that you are excited about your future in this walk with the Lord. You may even be thinking I want to do great things for the Lord. We often relate to this as being on fire for the Lord.

At this point, I must warn you that you in and of yourself can do nothing for the Lord. He is developing you so that He can do His will through you. He wants you to be like a piece of clay in the potter's hand.

Isaiah 64:8 *But now, O LORD, thou art our father; we are the clay, and thou our potter; and we all are the work of thy hand.*

You do not want to let that fire for the Lord go out. The consequences would not be good.

Revelations 3:15-16 *I know thy works, that thou art neither cold nor hot: I would thou wert cold or hot. So then because thou art lukewarm, and neither cold nor hot, I will spew thee out of my mouth.*

So far you have been following a plan outlined in this book. Now you must adopt a plan for yourself to continue learning. If you do not you run the risk of losing that fire that burns within and begin to fall back or backslide. Without continual study of the Bible, you will not have the necessary tools to enable your faith to grow.

How do you put together a proper Bible study plan? One way is to do a topical study. Find a topic, gather all the verses you can find on that topic, and then follow step four in the instruction section of this book.

The best way, in my opinion, if it is feasible, is to enroll into a Bible School or University. They will supply the topics and start you on the right track, they can also answer any questions you may come up with, or they can give you the information you need to find the answer yourself.

Why does it take so much time to prepare yourself to follow Gods leading? Like all of God's creations, plants and animals, you have to grow. Peter tells us, .

1 Peter 2:2,3 *As newborn babes, desire the sincere milk of the word, that ye may grow thereby:*

3If so be ye have tasted that the Lord is gracious.

Consider the giant oak tree. It starts as an acorn (seed) that must be planted and watered to grow. That acorn had to die so the tree could begin to grow.

John 12:24 Verily, verily, I say unto you, Except a corn of wheat fall into the ground and die, it abideth alone: but if it die, it bringeth forth much fruit.

It is the same with you, you must die unto yourself so Christ can grow in you. This growth will take time. I cannot tell you how much time as each person is different.

John 3:30 He must increase, but I must decrease.

What this means is that you must humble yourself. You must not depend on yourself for anything. Faith in Jesus and what He did on the cross, and is the only way for you to grow and be fruitful.

1 Peter 5:6 Humble yourselves therefore under the mighty hand of God, that he may exalt you in due time:

After you planted that acorn you can see a small oak shoot coming up. In time it grows a few leaves. After a little more time, it has grown into a small tree and starts to bear a few acorns. But it will be several years before it becomes a giant oak tree and produces bushels of acorns. This is the same with you. God wants to use you. Just do not get in a hurry. If you are obedient to Him and continue to study that time will come. This is where the fruit of patience comes in.

Psalms 27:14 Wait on the LORD: be of good courage, and he shall strengthen thine heart: wait, I say, on the LORD.

SECTION FOUR
America at the Tipping Point

Chapter 16
Introduction

I was sitting at my computer a few days ago thinking about the statement, "if you do not learn from the past, you are doomed to repeat it" by George Santayana. It was at this time that the Lord gave me the idea to write a book that would compare the United States of America to Israel. Why Israel? Because when you study each of them, you can see the same mistakes Israel made that the United States of America is making. The mistakes Israel made cost them their country. Could these mistakes lead to our demise?

It is my prayer that we will see our mistakes, humble ourselves, and repent of our ways. This will open the door for God to once again shower His blessings upon us, and continue to use the USA to spread the gospel around the world.

Israel had God's promise to bring their country back from their isolation. The United States of America does not have that promise. Once we are gone there is little hope we will ever return.

I believe the Lord intended this book to be a warning to America to turn from the direction we are traveling. What direction is that? We are turning away from the teaching of the Bible, and doing that which is right in our own eyes. America needs to return to a position of following God's commandments or face His wrath. Please read this section carefully and let God speak to your heart.

Chapter 17

ISRAEL

The nation of Israel began when God told Abram (Abraham) to leave his home in Haran and go to Canaan.

Genesis 12:1-4 Now the LORD had said unto Abram, Get thee out of thy country, and from thy kindred, and from thy father's house, unto a land that I will shew thee:

2 And I will make of thee a great nation, and I will bless thee, and make thy name great; and thou shalt be a blessing:

3 And I will bless them that bless thee, and curse him that curseth thee: and in thee shall all families of the earth be blessed.

4 So Abram departed, as the LORD had spoken unto him; and Lot went with him: and Abram was seventy and five years old when he departed out of Haran.

Why did God choose Abram to be the father of a new country? Abram may have had higher moral standards than his friends and neighbors, but this was not the reason God chose him. God chose him because He wanted to choose him. when God spoke to him, he listened; when God promised, he trusted; when God commanded, he obeyed. God is sovereign, He is also omniscient, knowing that Abram would do what God instructed him to do and that was enough for him to be chosen. God wanted a nation

He could use to bring us His Word, and the Messiah. The following verse describes what God wanted.

Exodus 19:5,6 *Now therefore, if ye will obey my voice indeed, and keep my covenant, then ye shall be a peculiar treasure unto me above all people: for all the earth is mine:*

6And ye shall be unto me a kingdom of priests, and an holy nation.

At the age of 100 God gave Abram a son, Issac. Issac begat Jacob, and Jacob begat the 12 sons that would become the heads of the twelve tribes of Israel.

Joseph was the eleventh son and was despised by the other 10. They ended up selling him into slavery. He ended up in Egypt where he found favor with the Pharaoh in power. Pharaoh made him second in command of all Egypt.

A famine settled over all the lands and food was very hard to come by. Jacob sent his sons to Egypt to buy provisions. Egypt had storehouses of grains as Joseph had stored all the excesses in the previous years. When the sons arrived in Egypt, to buy food, Joseph recognized them, but he never let them know who he was. Through some trickery Joseph got the sons to convince Jacob and the youngest son to move to Egypt where they would have sufficient food and grazing for their livestock. They spent the next 430 years in Egypt and become a very large group of people.

Pharaoh had kept the Hebrews in slavery for most of the 430 years. It was now time to leave and become a nation of their own. Pharaoh was not in favor of this plan, so God raised Moses up to lead them out. Moses approached Pharaoh 9 times asking him to release the

Hebrews. Each time pharaoh declined and God struck the Egyptians with a plague. The tenth time God killed the firstborn of every living thing in Egypt. The Hebrews were spared these plagues. At that time Pharaoh relented and allowed the Hebrews to leave.

This was the beginning of the Hebrews as the nation of Israel, and of the sins Israel began to make. It took 47 days for them to travel from Goshen to Mount Sinai. The first leg of the trip was from Goshen to the Red Sea where they set up camp. They stayed 8 days in this camp. During that time, they were able to look back on their trial and see the Pharaoh and his army pursuing them.

In front of them was the Red Sea which also wrapped around one side with a large mountain range on the other side. They were trapped. They began complaining that Moses had brought them out into the desert to be killed.

It had been just about three weeks since they were spared, by God, from the angel of death. Do you think that they should have looked to God to deliver them? They were guilty of not trusting God. Moses prayed and God had him stretch his staff over the waters and the waters opened allowing the Israelite's to cross on dry ground. They crossed the Red Sea on the 25th day. Upon reaching the other side they saw Pharaoh still following. While Pharaoh and his army were in the middle, God let the waters return and killed every one of the Egyptians. There was a great party and songs, led by Merriam, thanking God for their safety.

During the next 22 days, they crossed the desert to Sinai. Three more times they rebelled against Moses for not having enough water, enough food, and no meat.

They still had not learned to trust God and call on Him for help. When they were crying about water and food they had not even run out, they were looking to the future. How could they not remember as great a miracle as crossing the Red Sea on dry ground, and not look to God for these necessities?

God did not overlook these sins, He allowed the Amalikites to attack them, but then He allowed them to attack the Amalikites. God will eventually punish you if you continue to ignore Him.

After reaching Sinai where they would camp for about a year. It was here that God told them that they would be His people.

Exodus 19:6 *And ye shall be unto me a kingdom of priests, and an holy nation. These are the words which thou shalt speak unto the children of Israel.*

God also came down the mountain and gave them the Ten Commandments verbally. He did this to let the people know that He was the one giving instructions to Moses so they would listen to Moses. After this, He called Moses back up the mountain where He wrote those 10 commandments on tablets of stone. Moses was gone for forty days and the people began to speculate that he was dead or had deserted them. Moses had left Aaron in charge and the people requested he make them a golden calf that they could worship. They are now not only guilty of not trusting God for their needs, but they became idol worshipers and adulterers of God.

During the time at Sinai God set up a government to govern the nation of Israel. He built the Tabernacle and initiated the priesthood. He gave the priesthood the job of taking down, transporting, and setting up the tabernacle at their campsites.

It was now time for Israel to take the next step in their journey. Sinai to Kadesh Barnea. This is where God had planned for them to enter the promised land. There was an easy way to Kadesh on an established road, and it would only take eleven days. As they watched the cloud over the tabernacle it began to move, but it set out across the desert in a different direction. The path was described as, "through a stony ravine and barren waste. A land of deserts and pits, a land of drought, and the shadow of death, a land that no man passed, and where no man dwelt".

After just three days the complaints and grumbling began again. Not only did they complain about the route but they again complained about needing meat. They not only blamed Moses, but began to question God's ability to provide meat.

This all took a heavy toll on Moses and he prayed to God once again that the burden was too much. God had him choose 70 men from the people to share the burden. Then, once again, God provided meat for the people. He told them it was not for just one or two days but for an entire month until it came out their noses. God then struck them with a plague.

After this, we see the introduction of a more serious sin, human pride. Merriam and Arron, who were sister and brother to Moses, and who had always been at his side, now complained that they had not been consulted in the appointment of the seventy and that Moses was being counseled by his father Jethro. Moses took them to the Tabernacle where God came down and smote Merriam with leprosy.

Arron who also was guilty of forming the golden calf, back at the Sinai camp, would receive his punishment later. Moses prayed, once again, for Merriam and after a week she was healed.

If Merriam's envy and pride had not been rebuked, by the Lord, the entire Israelite population would have become impossible with more complaints and disrespect. We should be very aware of this in our own lives. Remember, God sees everything, not only in the present but also in the future. When He corrects us, it is for our good. Even when it is uncomfortable. He does everything perfectly.

Israel spent 3 months traveling from Sinai to Kadesh. This information was supplied from "Chronology of the Forty Years in the Wilderness" by Julian Spriggs M.A.

Upon reaching Kadesh God instructed Moses to send out twelve spies, one from each tribe, to spy out the land. When they returned, from their trip, ten of the men stated that the land was truly flowing with milk and honey, but the cities were walled and there were giants in the land, and the Israelites could not defeat them.

The two remaining spies, Joshua and Caleb stated that God would give them the victory. The people took the word of the ten men and refused to proceed. Again, they did not consult God and did not believe that He would give them victory. This led to rebellion and God punished them by making them stay in the desert for 38 more years, until all those over 20 were dead. They would never see the promised land. Of the entire group, Caleb and Joshua are the only two who had the opportunity to enter the promised land.

Kadash to Jordan River.

It took just over 20 months for the Israelis to make the trip from Kadash to the Jordan. They had planned to take the Kings Hi-Way through Edom, but Edom refused them direct passage., as did the Amorites. Instead of an easy walk-through lush land they once again had to circumvent those countries and travel through the rough, dry, and rocky desert. This entailed their return to the Red Sea and then around Edom and Moab.

This track took them to Mt. Hor. Upon reaching Mt. Hor God commanded Moses to Take Aaron and his son Eleazar to the top of the Mt. where Aaron was to pass his duties on to his son. Aaron then died and was buried on the Mountain. He never got to see the promised land. This was the result of his previous sins.

As Israel continued the trek, they encountered defeat by Arad one of the Canaanite kings. However, as they sought God's help, they were able to defeat that army. They now found themselves, once again in a hot, sandy valley, destitute of shade or vegetation. They suffered weariness and thirst. In all this they remained true to form and blamed God and Moses for their troubles.

Because of their continuous infidelity, and lack of confidence in God, God sent fiery snakes to bite them. Many died and many were extremely sick and about to die. The people repented and admitted their sins before God and Moses. Moses was given instructions to make an image of a snake and set it on a pole. As the people looked up to the serpent they were saved. This is a picture of people today looking up to Jesus, by faith, and being saved.

From this point the Israelis had to pass through the area controlled by King Sihon. Moses sent messengers to King Sihon of the Amorites, asking his permission for the children of Israel to pass through his land. Moses promised to use only the highway and to make full reparations for any damage that might ensue. They would purchase their food and water from the local people.

Sihon refused this request and mobilized his entire army against the children of Israel. Sihon was defeated, and the children of Israel took possession of his entire country. We should take note here that King Sihon's people were superior to the Israelis, as a fighting people, and were more experienced at war. this goes to show that if God is on your side you will succeed.

The next king to challenge Israel was Og, the giant king of Bashan. He too was vanquished and slain by Moses, and his land passed into the hands of the children of Israel.

These two battles show that if God has given you a task, He will provide whatever is necessary to see you can complete that task

Both nations were part of Canaan. The land was perfect for raising cattle and sheep. Reuben, Gad, and the Half Tribe of Manasseh requested that they take possession of their portion of what God promised them in that conquered land on this side of the Jordan. They promised to cross the Jordan and fight with Joshua to take possession of the rest of Canaan, only to return to their families when the fighting was done. Moses agreed with this.

Shittim

Shittim is a large area in the plains of Moab directly across from Jericho, immediately east of the Jordan and north of the Dead Sea. Shittim is significant in Israel's history because it is the site of the last encampment of the nation of Israel at the end of the 38 years in the wilderness. This was just before crossing the Jordan into the Promised Land.

In Shittim, the Israelites were enticed into idolatrous Baal worship and immoral sexual relations with Moabite and Midianite women. Angered by their unfaithfulness, the Lord sent a plague on the men of Israel, killing twenty-four thousand of them.

From this camp Moses was able to see across the Jordan and see the promised land. He requested of God that he be able to enter the land. God would not change His mind. He instructed Moses to climb to the top of Mt. Pisgah where he would be able to see the land. After turning over command to Joshua, Moses died. His grave was never found.

After wandering in the desert for 40 years, the Israelites finally approached the boundary of the Promised Land near Shittim. Their great leader Moses had died, and God had transferred power to Moses' successor, Joshua.

Joshua moved the Israelis from Shittim to the edge of the Jordan. Then Joshua told the Israelites the following.

Joshua said to the Israelites, "Come here and listen to the words of the Lord your God. This is how you will know that the living God is among you and that he will certainly drive out before you the Canaanites, Hittites, Hivites, Perizzites, Girgashites, Amorites and Jebusites. The ark of the covenant of the Lord of all the earth will go into the Jordan ahead of you. And as soon as the priests who were carrying the ark of the Lord set foot in the Jordan, its waters, flowing downstream, will be cut off and stand up in a heap."

When the people broke camp to cross the Jordan, the priests carrying the ark of the covenant went ahead of them. Now the Jordan is at flood stage all during harvest. Yet as soon as the priests who carried the ark reached the Jordan and their feet touched the water's edge, the water from upstream stopped flowing. It piled up in a heap a great distance away, at a town called Adam in the vicinity of Zaretan, while the water flowing down to the Sea of the Arabah (that is, the Dead Sea) was completely cut off. The people crossed over opposite Jericho. The priests who carried the ark of the covenant stopped in the middle of the Jordan and stood on dry ground, backs to the heap, while all Israel passed by until the whole nation had completed the crossing on dry ground.

When the whole nation had finished crossing the Jordan, the Lord said to Joshua, "Choose twelve men from among the people, one from each tribe, and tell them to take up twelve stones from the middle of the Jordan, from right where the priests are standing, and carry them over with you and put them down at the place where you stay tonight. Joshua called together the twelve men he had appointed from the Israelites, one from each tribe, and said to them, "Go over before the ark of the Lord your God into the middle of the Jordan. Each of you is to take up a stone on his shoulder, according to the number of the tribes of the Israelites, to serve as a sign among you. In the future, when your children ask you, 'What do these stones mean?' tell them that the flow of the Jordan was cut off before the ark of the covenant of the Lord. When it crossed the Jordan, the waters of the Jordan were cut off. These stones are to be a memorial to the people of Israel forever."

Now the priests who carried the ark remained standing in the middle of the Jordan until everything the Lord had commanded Joshua was done by the people, just as Moses had directed Joshua. The people hurried over, and as soon as all of them had crossed, the ark of the Lord and the priests came to the other side while the people watched.

There are two very important lessons to be learned from the crossing of the Jordan.

1. When the Lord gives you a task He will wait until you make the first move. The water did not stop flowing until the priest's feet were in the water.

2. The Lord will then proceed ahead of you as you begin His assigned task. The priests and the Ark went first! He will then stand between you and any danger while you do His task. The Priests and the Ark took a position in the middle of the stream and between the heap of water and the people. He will then proceed behind you, continuing to protect your rear.

The Israelis then set up camp in Gilgal

Gilgal was a place of consecration and change. It was at Gilgal that the Israelites were circumcised and celebrated their first Passover in the Promised Land. The children of those who had wandered in the desert had not yet been circumcised, and it was time for them to take the sign of the covenant and be set apart as God's people. This time of circumcision is what gave Gilgal its name, for the Lord said He had "rolled away the reproach of Egypt from you." The reproach was the uncircumcised condition; the "rolling away" of that reproach set them apart, once and for all, from the Egyptian people and that way of life. After the Israelites celebrated the Passover and began to eat the produce of their new land, the manna that the Lord had provided the Israelites during their years of wandering stopped.

Joshua now began the conquest of Canaan with the city of Jerico being first. During the conquest of Canaan, God intervened miraculously on several occasions, including the day the sun stood still (Joshua 10). Israel was largely successful in defeating or driving out the Canaanites; however, they were not completely successful. Sometimes they left pockets of Canaanites to continue to rule themselves, and sometimes they enslaved the Canaanites. Both things had been forbidden by God, who told Israel to drive them out completely. As a result, the Canaanites remained in the land and became a temptation and a snare to the people of Israel. At times Israel would worship the Canaanites' gods, and because of this God would allow those remaining pagans to rule over them.

Many years later, after the Lord had given peace to Israel and all its surrounding enemies, Joshua had become very old, Joshua called together all of Israel, including their leaders, officials, judges, and tribal officers. He told them, "I am old now after having lived many years.

You have seen everything that the Lord your God has done to all of these nations on your behalf because it has been the Lord your God who has been fighting on your behalf. Now look, I have allocated these nations that remain as an inheritance for your tribes, including all of the nations that I have eliminated, from the Jordan River to the Mediterranean[Sea to the west. The Lord your God will expel them in front of you, driving them out of your sight. You will take possession of this land, just as the Lord your God promised you. Stand very strong, then, so you can obey and carry out everything written in the Book of the Law of Moses, turning neither to the right nor the left of it. That way, you will not mingle with those nations, that remain among you, nor mention the name of their gods, nor make oaths by them, nor serve them, nor worship them. Instead, you are to hold fast to the Lord your God, as you have done today because the Lord has expelled great and strong nations ahead of you. Now as for you, not a single man has been able to oppose you right to this day. A single man makes a thousand flee because the Lord your God is the one who is fighting for you, just as he promised you. Be very diligent to love the Lord your God, because if you ever turn back and cling to those who remain of these nations by intermarrying with them and associating one with another, know for certain that the Lord your God will not continue to drive out these nations ahead of you. Instead, they will be a snare and a trap for you, a whip to your backs, and thorns in your eyes, until you perish from this good land that the Lord your God has given you.

"Look here: today I am going down the path that everyone on earth takes, and you know with all your hearts and souls that not a single word of all the good things that the Lord your God spoke about you has failed to happen. Everything has been fulfilled not one of them has failed. However, just as all the good things have come about that the Lord your God promised, so also the Lord will bring upon you all the threats until he has destroyed you from possessing this good land that he has given you. When you break the covenant of the Lord your God that he commanded you to obey by going to serve other gods and worship them, then the anger of the Lord will blaze against you, and you will perish quickly from this good land that he gave you."

It is important here, that you take note of all the things the Lord has told the Israelis not to do, but they would always begin doing them later. Each new generation that came along, would go back to doing what the Lord had told them not to do. All the promises that God gave them, He kept. Not one did He fail to do.

This pattern continued throughout the rest of Israel's time as a country. Through the time of the judges, where God would allow them to be captured and turned to servitude. When the people repented and cried out to God He would raise a judge to defeat the captor and restore them to their rightful place.

They got tired of the judges and requested that God give them a king like the countries around them. God told them what a king would demand of them, but they insisted and they got their king. Some of those kings did what was right in the eyes of the Lord, but many did not. You will see as you study Israel through time that the people followed the direction that the king went in. After the third king, God split the tribes into two countries. Ten of the tribes became the country of Israel and two as the country of Judah.

Israel never had a king who did what was right in the eyes of the Lord. As a result, Israel was defeated, taken into captivity, and never came back as a country. Judah, on the other hand, had some good kings. When a bad one came along God would allow them to be defeated and serve the captor in servitude. When they repented and cried out to the Lord, He would reestablish them. God did this due to His promise to Abraham, Issac, and Jacob.

Finally, they became so bad that God let them be captured by the king of Babylon where they were sent into captivity for the next 70 years. After Babylon was captured by the Persians, they allowed the Israelis to return and rebuild Jerusalem and the temple. For the next four hundred years God is silent until the birth of John the Baptist and Jesus.

At that time the Israelis were under the control of the Roman Empire. The ruling heads of Israel, and the people, rejected Jesus and had Him crucified. The Romans then, in seventy AD, destroyed Jerusalem, the Temple, and killed many of the Jewish people. The rest were scattered around the world for the next 2000 years without a country.

Chapter 18

AMERICA
The Greatest Country in the World Today

Why would I say that America is the greatest country in the world today? What makes America the greatest country in the world? Is it because we created more wealth than any other country? Is it because we have exceptional freedoms? Is it because we helped more countries and people around the world than any other country? Or is it because we have the strongest military? I could continue with these questions and most of them would be true to some extent, but I do not think that is the main reason for our position in the world. A country is only as good and strong as the men who founded it, and the system they set up to guide it.

If we look at Israel in the Old Testament days, we will see Israel was created, by God, through special men, for a specific purpose. To give His law and bring us the Messiah. For most of that time, they were the greatest country in the world. From Abraham to King David and all the others who played a part in Israel's history were exceptional men. While none of them were perfect their intent was. They accepted God's direction by faith and followed His commandments. As long as Israel's leadership did what was right in the sight of the Lord, the people followed and the nation prospered. When they did that which was evil in the sight of the Lord, the country fell away from God and the people began worshiping idols, the result was the country deteriorated. Eventually, because of the leadership and the people's failure to follow His commandments, and after numerous warnings, God let Israel be destroyed. In 70 AD Rome destroyed the temple along with Jerusalem. Many of the people were killed and the rest scattered around the world for the next 2000 years.

The USA was also started by exceptional men. These men were from countries that were ruled by kings and monarchies that demanded the people follow their religious laws. These men began a movement that brought many to the American shores where they formed the first colonies. All the men who helped found and establish America as a country, I am sure, were directed by God whether they were aware of it or not. (My opinion) I have a book, copyright 1883 by G. S Weaver, D.D. That speaks of their special qualities for the task at hand. See it below.

THE QUALITY OF COLONIAL MEN.

The colonial school of America was rough, but solid and genuine; and trained a people such as the world never saw before, as the seed of a new nation and a new era of mankind.

In re-studying the lessons of that school nothing is clearer than that the men of the colonies were superior to the men of the British parliament with whom they contended. They were better students of English law and history, and especially better in the principles of the English constitution. They were better philosophers; more acute and comprehensive in their view of government;

more loyal to reason and the lessons of human nature, and greatly more faithful in the application of Christian principles to human affairs. The debates in parliament, compared with the speeches in public meetings in the colonies, indicate clearly that the leaders, in thought, in the colonies were the profounder and better men. And the people's appreciation and acceptance of that thought, compared with the prevailing style of thought among the English people, showed that the masses of the colonial people had gained upon the people of the mother country by their hard colonial school. They had a clearer hold upon principles and a greater loyalty to them; knew and appreciated human rights better, and were truer to them; carried with a heartier faith the teachings of the Christian religion to their practical results, and believed more in individual responsibility and power. The result was, that both leaders and people became more assured in the righteousness of their convictions, and more positive in maintaining them. They became a people of thinkers who acted on their thoughts. Freedom, human rights, personal responsibility, the authority of rulers, the duties of people, were themes they studied and discussed. And this study had developed a power among the leaders able to cope with any English parliament, and among the people a stalwartness of conviction and will, superior to what prevailed among the English people."

Let us look at some of these men, the ones who designed the blueprint for America, and who signed the Declaration of Independence. Who were they? What kind of men were they? Twenty-four were lawyers and jurists. Eleven were merchants, nine were farmers and large plantation owners, men of means, well educated. But they signed the

Declaration of Independence knowing full well that the penalty would be death if they were captured.

Have you ever wondered what happened to the 56 men who signed the Declaration of Independence? Five signers were captured by the British as traitors, and tortured before they died. Twelve had their homes ransacked and burned. Two lost their sons in the revolutionary army, another had two sons captured. Nine of the 56 fought and died from wounds or hardships of the Revolutionary War. They signed and they pledged their lives, their fortunes, and their sacred honor. 30 of the 56 suffered grave consequences for the signature they made that fateful day. These gallant and brave men did not get involved to fill their pockets with the taxpayer's money. Their only reason was to do what was best for the people and the country regardless of the cost. How do you compare that to today's politicians?

We see the same qualities in the men who God used to build Israel. We do not have to name them as they are listed in the Bible. Strong men who followed God's law, did what was best for the people and country.

Why did God bring about the formation of America? I believe (my opinion) it was to build a strong country that followed God's direction, who then, using the wealth of America, began to bring the Gospel to the rest of the world.

What country sends, by far, the most missionaries to the world. America still tops the chart in terms of total missionaries sent. America sent 127,000 missionaries in 2010 compared to the 34,000 sent by No. 2-ranked Brazil. However, we have not completed our task. We must continue to send our people around the world until all have heard the good news of Jesus Christ. To accomplish this, we must turn our country around from its headlong rush to destruction.

So, what made America the greatest nation in the world today? Exceptional men, who wrote the Declaration of Independence and the Constitution of the United States. These people, and those two papers gave the power of government to the people and made it possible for a person, who had the intelligence and fortitude, to build huge corporations creating jobs and wealth. Along with those corporations, anyone could attempt to fulfill their dreams and have their own business. The combination of those two freedoms made this country a success and made it possible to grow the wealth that enabled us to become the greatest country in the world. With the freedom to pursue God and their dreams.

If we take this ability away from those empire-builders, we will destroy the very fabric of our nation. I believe the keywords that make it all work are as follows. "We hold these Truths to be self-evident, that all Men are created equal, that they are endowed by their Creator with certain unalienable Rights, that among these are Life, Liberty, and the Pursuit of Happiness."

But I believe the greatest reason for our standing, in the world, is that the men who founded this country were men who believed in God. They mostly believed the Bible was the Word of God, and formed our laws on biblical principles. For this God has graciously blessed this country.

While the Bible does not speak of America, it does tell us that God will bless those who walk in His ways. The fact that the founders all had a strong belief in God, and patterned our laws on biblical principles, has everything to do with what this country became. We must continue to follow God's statutes and commandments. The very survival of our nation depends on it.

God has blessed this country over and over. From the war for independence through the Second World War, He gave us the ability to come out on top. That is not to say that everything this country has done or is doing, is correct. He has just rewarded us for what we did right. Be sure of one thing, He will not overlook the sinful ways that are taking place today. He is not just the God of love; He is also the God of justice. The following verse lets you know that God will not stand by and do nothing forever.

Romans 1:24 *Wherefore God also gave them up to uncleanness through the lusts of their own hearts, to dishonor their own bodies between themselves: 25 Who changed the truth of God into a lie, and worshipped and served the creature more than the Creator, who is blessed forever. Amen.*

Since the Declaration of Independence through WW2, the United States was involved in 6 major wars, excluding the American Civil War. During that time God gave us the ability to win every one of them. His hand remained on us. When you give a little effort to follow His commandments He gives you, in return, blessings beyond your efforts.

Since WW2 we have been in 5 major wars. We have not won even one of those. Why? I believe it all started during WW2. The women were pulled into the manufacturing of war armaments. Before that, they mostly stayed home and raised the children. Most of the people lived in the country during those times.

Now, because jobs were in the cities we became

an urban community. In the country, the children had chores they were responsible for so they did not have a lot of free time to get into trouble. The moms and dads also taught them respect. In the cities, those things all went away. The kids were left on their own or someone else took care of them, those caretakers did not care as much for them as the moms did. The result is they never learned the necessity to provide for their wants or respect for others. They began to expect everything to be given to them. With the free time they gained, they began getting into trouble. They no longer respected authority and they began doing what they deemed right in their own eyes. What were the results?

Sexual freedom!

This was the beginning of the hippy movement. If it feels good, do it. Casual sex became common. They mistakenly took the pleasure of sex as love. They married the wrong person and then learned that they did not love each other and got divorced. All the free sex and divorces left us with children who had to be raised with only one parent. They lost an important role model. What does the Bible teach about casual sex?

1Corinthians 6:18 *Flee fornication. Every sin that a man doeth is without the body; but he that committeth fornication sinneth against his own body.*

We find those kids had traditional rules thrown out, and in their place, they made their own. There was very little respect for authority and they did what was right in their own eyes. This is what we have today and these are the people that are now beginning to run our country.

The following are the results of that way of thinking.

Bible and prayer were taken out of schools and government.

On June 25, 1962, the United States Supreme Court decided in 'Engel v. Vitale that a prayer approved by the New York Board of Regents for use in schools violated the First Amendment by constituting an establishment of religion. The following year, in Abington School District v. Schempp, the Court disallowed Bible readings in public schools for similar reasons. These two landmark Supreme Court decisions centered on the place of religion in public education, particularly the place of Protestantism, which had long been accepted as the given American faith tradition. Both decisions ultimately changed the face of American civil society.

The separation of church and state then began to filter into government. The Ten Commandments, and other like scripture, were taken out of government offices. What does the Bible say about the separation of church and state?

Mark 12.30 *And thou shalt love the Lord thy God with all thy heart, and with all thy soul, and with all thy mind, and with all thy strength: this is the first commandment.*

Romans 13:1-2 *Let every soul be subject unto the higher powers. For there is no power but of God: the powers that be are ordained of God.2 Whosoever therefore resisteth the power, resisteth the ordinance of God: and they that resist shall receive to themselves damnation.*

Abortion

In 1973 abortion was legalized with the Supreme courts ruling on the Roe vs Wade lawsuit. What does the Bible say?

Leviticus 18:21 *And thou shalt not let any of thy seed pass through the fire to Molech, neither shalt thou profane the name of thy God: I am the LORD.*

Molech was a large, hollow, brass idol. It was so designed to be able to hold a child in its hands and arms. A fire was then kindled inside of it. The Idol would turn cherry red with heat and burn the child to death.

Homosexuality

Same-sex marriage. June 26, 2015, marks a major milestone for civil rights in the United States, as the Supreme Court announced its decision in Obergefell v. Hodges. By one vote, the court ruled that same-sex marriage cannot be banned in the United States and that all same-sex marriages must be recognized nationwide, finally granting same-sex couples equal rights to heterosexual couples under the law.

What the bible says.

Leviticus 18:22 *Thou shalt not lie with mankind, as with womankind: it is abomination.*

These are just some of the major law's contrary to scripture. I am sure there are more.

This gives you a small insight into where we are in this country today as opposed to our beginning.

Chapter 19

Comparisons, Israel, and America

What was Israel's main fault as they left Egypt on their way to the promised land? They failed to look to God for their needs and protection and did not obey His commandments.

Israel had just left Egypt. God had just punished Egypt with 10 plagues for not taking heed to God's command to (let my people go.) They had to know those plagues were to convince Pharaoh to let them go. Yet just a few days later, when they were blocked at the Red Sea, and Pharaoh was following them, they failed to remember all He had just done for them in Egypt. They were looking for their own solution to save themselves. Then when they were running out of food or water, as they traveled to Sinai, did they look to God. NO! They still blamed Moses. Then they had Aaron make them a golden calf at Sinai. God had allowed the tribulations on their journey to teach them to look to Him for their needs.

What do we do here in America when we need help? Who do we turn to? We start looking for a better job that will pay more so we can buy those items, or look for someone that can help us. Has God not told us that He will meet our need

Philippians 4:19 *But my God shall supply all your need according to his riches in glory by Christ Jesus.*

Matthew 6:26 *Behold the fowls of the air: for they sow not, neither do they reap, nor gather into barns; yet your heavenly Father feedeth them. Are ye not much better than they?*

Now we need to understand. Those verses don't mean He is going to give you all your desires, riches, or wants. Although He could. He will meet your needs, not your wants. If you are walking in His will your wants will be in line with His will. Your wants will be the same as His.

James 4:3 *Ye ask, and receive not, because ye ask amiss, that ye may consume it upon your lusts.*

Israel's next fault was Idol worship. Remember when they were camped at Mt. Sinai and Moses was up on the mountain 40 days and nights? They had Aaron make them a Golden calf that they could pray to as they did in Egypt.

Exodus 32:2-4 *And Aaron said unto them, Break off the golden earrings, which are in the ears of your wives, of your sons, and of your daughters, and bring them unto me.*

4And he received them at their hand, and fashioned it with a graving tool, after he had made it a molten calf: and they said, these be thy gods, O Israel, which brought thee up out of the land of Egypt.

What are our idols in America? Is it wealth, houses, cars? There are hundreds of them. Anything you desire more than you desire God is an Idol. He must be your main desire over anything else. Do we come anywhere close to that in this country? If we want a closer walk with our God, we must allow Him to direct our paths.

They sacrificed their children to idols. When Solomon was king the Israelis started sacrificing their children to Moloch. Do you think God looks at abortion any differently today than He did then? That baby in the womb is just as much alive as it is when it is born. If it were not alive the cells could not grow. Life came through the parents when God breathed life into Adams's nostrils at creation. That is when life began.

Genesis 2:7 *And the LORD God formed man of the dust of the ground, and breathed into his nostrils the breath of life; and man became a living soul.*

Israel committed Fornication and adultery. remember at the camp in Shittim.

Numbers 25:1 *And Israel abode in Shittim, and the people began to commit whoredom with the daughters of Moab.*

Do you think this is any worse than what is happening in America today? Fornication is an everyday event. It is in all our movies, TV, and ads. The dictionary definition of fornication. (Consensual sexual intercourse between two persons not married to each other.)

Adultery. God is not just talking about the sexual side of adultery. He refers to it also as spiritual adultery. We are all guilty of this and deserve his judgment for it. Thankfully Jesus paid the penalty for this and much more. His love is stronger than our sin.

James 4:4 *Ye adulterers and adulteresses, know ye not that the friendship of the world is enmity with God? whosoever therefore will be a friend of the world is the enemy of God.*

Do you see that we are just as guilty as Israel was? Eventually, Israel lost their country for some 2000 years. Luckily for them, they have a promise, from God, to bring them back. We do not have that promise. Once we are gone the future is bleak.

We need to fall on our knees, repent, and ask God to help us return to the country we used to be. How does God see us today? Just like He saw the Israelis then.

Isaiah 64:6 *But we are all as an unclean thing, and all our righteousnesses are as filthy rags, and we all do fade as a leaf; and our iniquities, like the wind, have taken us away.*

Isaiah was writing to the Israeli people, but this verse can be applied to us today also.

Romans 3:23 *For all have sinned, and come short of the glory of God;*

There is no difference between the Israelis and us today. The only difference now is that God, in His love and mercy, sent His son, Jesus Christ to pay the penalty for our sins and sinful ways. When God looks at us now, He sees us through the Blood that Jesus shed on the cross.

Chapter 20
TO THE POLITICIANS

What do the American people want in a politician? The first thing that comes to mind is a person who takes their job seriously. An honest person who will do their job to better the country, and the people, and not to fill their own pockets, and their lust for prominence. They should have the values of those who first formed our government. They need to be reliable, educated, and have a heart to better the country. Men who fit the description of those mentioned earlier in this book, (The Quality of Colonial Men) Thomas Jefferson tells it this way. ("I have the consolation of having added nothing to my private fortune during my public service, and of retiring with hands clean as they are empty.") We see today many who entered office with very little and retired with millions. I do not think that shows an attitude of bettering the country or the people.

The founding fathers did not take office to improve themselves financially or for their recognition. It is a serious thing to take the responsibility of leading the people and to show the world that we can be trusted.

Since it has been proven that this country was created and governed by Christian principles made us the richest and most trusted country in the world. It should continue in that direction. We cannot continue to pass legislation that is in direct opposition to God's commandments. This would just lead us down the same path that Israel followed, which cost them their country for over 2000 years.

The Lord has blessed this country because we started following His commandments. If we will but do this, He gives us a huge promise in the Bible.

Deuteronomy 28;1 *And it shall come to pass, if thou shalt hearken diligently unto the voice of the LORD thy God, to observe and to do all his commandments which I command thee this day, that the LORD thy God will set thee on high above all nations of the earth:*

What a great promise. Up through WW2, He did just that for us. I would suggest that you read all Deuteronomy chapter 28 in its entirety. The chapter is sixty-eight verses long. The first fourteen verses are God's promise to you. The next fifty-four tells the consequences if you fail to follow them. While this was written to the Israeli people, just as in other parts of the Bible, it can be applied to us as well.

God has blessed this country, as He said He would, in the first fourteen verses of Deuteronomy 28. The problem is that we are turning away from His commandments, and are moving in the wrong direction. Today's government is beginning to fall away from those commandments very quickly. We are beginning to see the results of our ignoring God's direction.

John Adams said this. ("Our Constitution was made only for a moral and religious people. It is wholly inadequate to the government of any other.")

Can we look at our country today and say it is a moral and religious country? I think not.

John Adams also said, ("Government is instituted for the common good; for the protection, safety, prosperity, and happiness of the people; and not for profit, honor, or private interest of any one man, family, or class of men; therefore, the people alone have an incontestable, unalienable, and indefeasible right to institute government; and to reform, alter, or totally change the same, when their protection, safety, prosperity, and happiness require it.")

George Washington's Quote ("It is impossible to govern the world without God. It is the duty of all nations to acknowledge the Providence of Almighty God, to obey his will, to be grateful for his benefits, and humbly implore his protection and favor.")

The government that is running things today does not seem to fit any of these quotes. They have moved away from the very principles of our founding fathers and God. It is an absolute necessity that we stop this now.

Let us look at early Israel and how their leaders affected the people and country. When a leader was doing what was right in the eyes of God, the people followed suit, and the country was blessed. When the leader was evil in the sight of the Lord again the people followed suit and the country, including the people, paid the price for their disloyalty. Many times, because of their turning away from Him, the country was invaded, and the people were taken hostage and turned to servitude. Because the Israelites were God's special people when they repented and cried out to the Lord for mercy, because He is a loving and merciful God, He would raise someone up to lead them back to their previous standing and they would once again enjoy a prosperous lifestyle.

The generation that repented and turned back to God's way of living continued to do so for the rest of their life. When the next generation came along, they would again start living life on their own terms. This cycle repeated itself time after time until finally in 70AD Rome destroyed Jerusalem and the temple. Many Jews were killed and the rest were scattered around the world for 2000 years without a country. If God would allow this to happen to His special people, what do you think He will do to us? Is this what our legislators want for America or has greed blinded them to what they are doing?

Isaiah spoke to the people and leadership of Israel and Judah in the following verses.

Isaiah 10:1-4 *Woe unto them that decree unrighteous decrees, and that write grievousness which they have prescribed;*

2 To turn aside the needy from judgment, and to take away the right from the poor of my people, that widows may be their prey, and that they may rob the fatherless!

3And what will ye do in the day of visitation, and in the desolation which shall come from far? to whom will ye flee for help? and where will ye leave your glory?

4Without me they shall bow down under the prisoners, and they shall fall under the slain. For all this his anger is not turned away, but his hand is stretched out still.

If you are a politician in America today, you need to read these verses very carefully.

Chapter 21

To Our Pastors

I believe that there are many pastors out there that are taking their job seriously. They are teaching what the Bible says and not what they want it to say.

Then many teach scripture as they interpret it, and not for what it says. It is taken out of context and they do not research it for the truth. They reason that they do not want to hurt their congregation. They worry that they might offend their audience and they may quit the church, thereby reducing their income.

The worst are those who are in it just for the money. They twist scripture to make the people feel good. They use any means to extract as much money as they can from their congregation as they possibly can.

God is not just a loving God He is also a just God and will meter out punishment where He believes it is necessary. Remember He holds those who are called to preach, to a higher standard than the average man, and you will be judged accordingly.

James 3:1 *My brethren, be not many masters, knowing that we shall receive the greater condemnation.*

In Hebrew, the word "master" can also be interpreted as "teacher". A pastor is a teacher. If you are not teaching all the Bible, to your congregation, you will be judged accordingly. Examine yourself and make sure you are teaching what God has called you to teach. If you do not, and some of the people in your congregation do not understand what the Bible teaches, and end up in eternal damnation, their blood will be on your hands and you will pay the price.

Make sure you are teaching what the Scriptures say, not what you think it says. Do not read or quote a scripture and add or subtract from it the way you think it should be. That is what the Pharisees did. Just go by what it says in the context it is written in. Paul told us that we see through a glass darkly. That means all people may not see it as you do. If you believe you are the only one who is right and everyone else is wrong, that is pride.

The Lord made this very clear to me. When I finished writing my third book I had a lot of free time on my hands. I decided I would use that time to study some of the doctrines that different churches believed. The first subject I chose was the rapture. Some believed it was before the tribulation. Others said it was post tribulation and others said it was mid tribulation.

To properly study this I had to place aside my own beliefs so I would not choose only those things I thought were correct. After a long period of study, I found that I could see each of the different beliefs and could see their reasoning for their beliefs. I turned to God in prayer and asked Him to help me see the correct way. Normally when I would ask God a question, I would find the answer in scripture or it would pop into my head sometime later.

This time His answer was immediate. He told me, "It does not matter if you are right or not. If you are wrong, it will not send you to hell. The only thing that is important is how you see Jesus". Then He reminded me of the incident in the Bible where the disciples came to Him about finding some others that were casting out devils in His name. They told those people to quit. Jesus answered in the following verse.

Mark 9:38-40 *And John answered him, saying, Master, we saw one casting out devils in thy name, and he followeth not us: and we forbad him because he followeth not us.39 But Jesus said, Forbid him not: for there is no man which shall do a miracle in my name, that can lightly speak evil of me.40 For he that is not against us is on our part.*

Then He reminded me of what Paul said about seeing things through a glass darkly.

1 Corinthians 13:12 *For now we see through a glass, darkly; but then face to face: now I know in part; but then shall I know even as also I am known.*

Now picture this in your mind. You are standing in front of a large tinted window. You can see only what is directly in front of you because the tinting blots out anything else. What you see causes you to conclude what the scene is. On the other side is someone else looking in. What he sees is a different part of the picture and He comes to a different conclusion. What you do not realize is that you are both looking at a small part of the same picture. You are not going to know what that picture looks like until you are in Heaven. You are both looking at the same picture, but because you cannot see it all you do not know the truth about what it says.

Because the other person does not see what you see it is not a reason to part ways. We are told to have unity in the church, and just because you have two different ideas of the picture is no reason to have nothing to do with that person or church. Love the Lord and your church, you need to have unity.

Ephesians 4:1-4 *I therefore, the prisoner of the Lord, beseech you that ye walk worthy of the vocation wherewith ye are called,2 With all lowliness and meekness, with longsuffering, forbearing one another in love;3 Endeavouring to keep the unity of the Spirit in the bond of peace.4 There is one body, and one Spirit, even as ye are called in one hope of your calling;*

Do not go off and start another church over a small disagreement. Love your brother and have fellowship with him. As the Lord told me, it does not matter, if you are wrong, it will not send you to hell. If I believe differently about something than some of the people around me believe. I do not hold that against them. I love them and enjoy fellowship with them.

Acts 1:13,14 *And when they were come in, they went up into an upper room, where abode both Peter, and James, and John, and Andrew, Philip, and Thomas, Bartholomew, and Matthew, James the son of Alphaeus, and Simon Zelotes, and Judas the brother of James.14 These all continued with one accord in prayer and supplication, with the women, and Mary the mother of Jesus, and with his brethren.*

John 17:20,21 *Neither pray I for these alone, but for them also which shall believe on me through their word;21 That they all may be one; as thou, Father, art in me, and I in thee, that they also may be one in us: that the world may believe that thou hast sent me.*

My prayer is that you live in unity as long as you know Jesus Christ.

Chapter 22

To The People

What can I do

This message is to every adult in the USA, regardless of race, religion, or creed. You must become like a piece of clay in the potter's hand. The clay has nothing to say about what the potter makes of it or how it is used.

Isaiah 64:8 *But now, O LORD, thou art our father; we are the clay, and thou our potter; and we all are the work of thy hand.*

The Lord wants us to let the Holy Spirit empty us of all our desires and wants and let Him work through us. This is not easy; I will have to admit I fight this constantly. We can do nothing for the Lord because all our righteousness is as filthy rags.

Isaiah 64:6 *But we are all as an unclean thing, and all our righteousnesses are as filthy rags; and we all do fade as a leaf; and our iniquities, like the wind, have taken us away.*

You also need to educate yourselves about the people running for office. That includes federal representatives, senators, or the president. It also includes your state representatives, senators, and governor. Also included are your district, county, and city officials. This is the only way you can keep control of your government. The country will go whichever way the leadership goes.

What can I do if the government begins to move away from the Constitution? Other than voting them out of office there is one more way you can go. Initiating a Convention of States. The Constitution gives us that right in Article V. (Article V of the U.S. Constitution gives states the power to call a Convention of States to propose amendments. It requires 34 states to call the convention and 38 states to ratify any proposed amendments.)

You can also look up your politician's website to see what they are all about, and you can look up their voting records so you can see what they believe. Yes, it will take some time, but the rewards will be worth it,

This convention can write amendments to the Constitution. One example, they can set term limits. You can get more information by typing "what is the convention of states" into your computer. If you do not have a computer most libraries have computers you can use. If you do not know how to do this ask your librarian and they can help you. You can also look up your politician's website to see what they are all about, and you can look up their voting records so you can see what they believe. Yes, it will take some time, but the rewards will be worth it, and God expects it.

Many of you consider yourselves Christians and you have the idea that you should not get involved in politics. That is not so. If you do not pay attention to who is being elected you may lose the things that make life worth living. We are instructed to pray for our leaders. Government was established by God at Sinai

1 Timothy 2:1 *I exhort therefore, that, first of all, supplications, prayers, intercessions, and giving of thanks, be made for all*

men;2 For kings, and for all that are in authority; that we may lead a quiet and peaceable life in all godliness and honesty.

Daniel 2:21 *And he changeth the times and the seasons: he removeth kings, and setteth up kings: he giveth wisdom unto the wise, and knowledge to them that know understanding:*

God is in control of who is in leadership. He places the good ones to bless us and the bad ones to teach and discipline us. He allows us the opportunity to share in those appointments through our prayers and our vote. God expects us to be knowledgeable about the people we vote into office. As we pray for His guidance in this, have faith that He will send you down the correct path to do His will.

You might want to review what you believe and why you believe it. The Bible tells us that not everyone who calls Jesus, Jesus will be saved. God looks at your heart to see if you are sincere.

James 2:19 *Thou believest that there is one God; thou doest well: the devils also believe, and tremble. 20But wilt thou know, O vain man, that faith without works is dead?*

A true Christian can be recognized by how he lives his life. When you accept Christ as your savior you become a new person. You will find that everything you do or say will be different, at least that is how it was with me. I recall coming home on leave. One of my old classmates told me that they talked about me in class. One of the guys said "I talked with him for quite a while and he never said a cuss word. Prior to my salvation, every other word was a swear word.

2 Corinthians 5:17 *Therefore if any man be in Christ, he is a new creature: old things are passed away; behold, all things are become new.*

In 1892 the Supreme Court declared that the USA was a Christian nation. If you want to question this look up what Justice David Josiah Brewer wrote in the court's brief in 1892. There are twelve pages of quotes and reasons he gave, to prove this decision. Even the King of England, in writing the charters for the expeditions that came to America, from Columbus to the Mayflower, listed one of the reasons for the expedition was to propagate the Gospel.

Why do I desire that you become a Christian? Because I know that God and Jesus Christ are real and that there is a God that guides us on this walk in life. You may question me as to how I can know this. Well, the answer may cause you to raise your eyebrows and question my sanity, but God has spoken to me in words I could hear.

To explain this, I must take you back to how I was raised.

I was raised by my mom and dad on a farm in Colorado. Dad was a Catholic, and Mom was a Protestant. To be married, in the Catholic church, my mom had to agree to raise the children as Catholics. That said, we rarely went to church. When we did, I never understood what was said. While I was aware that there was a Heaven and Hell, and a God, I never thought about it. I never wondered where I was going after I died. I do not recall ever having one of those thoughts cross my mind.

I left school in the middle of my junior year and went into the Navy. I eventually was shipped to the Philippines. I was stationed at a small Naval Air Station on the south side of Manila Bay called Sangley Point. It was a small peninsula. Along one side of the base was a beautiful sandy beach. The area of that beach, next to my hut, was used very seldom. There was never anyone on it at night. I used to go out at night to just walk and admire the beauty of the stars.

One night as I walked, enjoying the beauty of the stars, I suddenly heard a voice saying, "If you die tonight you will go to hell". I immediately began looking for the person who said it, but there was no one there. Somehow I knew that it was a message from God. Try to imagine what would go through your mind under the same circumstances. My immediate thought was, well I have been a Catholic all this time so this Sunday I will go to the protestant service and see if it makes a difference. Please note this is not meant to be a slam against Catholicism, these are just the thoughts that went through my mind. After the service, I thought," Well I didn't get anything from that service either, I need to look further.

As I exited the chapel, I noticed one of my squadron mates standing on the steps. I went over to him and said hi. He said he was waiting for some people that would pick him up. They would take him to their home with others from the base, they would play some games, have lunch, and service afterward. I thought that sounded like a fun way to spend the afternoon so I decided to wait and see if they would invite me also, and they did. It happened to be the Overseas Christian Serviceman's Center missionary. I went along and after going there for a few more times I accepted Jesus Christ as my Lord and Savior.

I was now a born-again Christian. Because God loved me so much, even though I was not deserving, He saved my soul as he is also willing to do for anyone who will repent and call on His name and put their faith in what He did on the Cross for you.

As soon as I stood up, after accepting Him, it felt as if the weight of the world was lifted from my shoulders. I was born again and all my sins were paid for by the blood of Jesus, those sins were the weight that was lifted from me.

I will talk about this some more in the next chapter. How you can find peace and joy in your life and be assured that you will spend eternity with Jesus your Savior, and your Father God. I can promise you that this is the answer to all the problems we face in life as an individual or country.

He gives us this time on earth to decide whether we will turn to Him or follow the ways of Satan. He wants our love and praise, but it would be of no value if it were not our choice to do so. Once we take our last breath, we no longer have the opportunity to make that choice. I would suggest that you also begin to seek the truth today. The Bible tells us that if we seek, we will find.

Matthew 7:7,8 *Ask, and it shall be given you; seek, and ye shall find; knock, and it shall be opened unto you:8 For every one that asketh receiveth; and he that seeketh findeth; and to him that knocketh it shall be opened.*

There is a way that Christians can help in this battle to prolong the life of America. Form a group in your church to study those who are seeking a place in government, along with those already in office, pray for them, and study who they are and what they stand for.

Timothy 2: 1-3 *I exhort therefore, that, first of all, supplications, prayers, intercessions, and giving of thanks, be made for all men; 2 For kings, and for all that are in authority; that we may lead a quiet and peaceable life in all godliness and honesty.3 For this is good and acceptable in the sight of God our Savior;*

Chapter 23
The Wrap Up

In this chapter, I want to review what we have covered up to now.

In the first chapter, we followed the Israeli nation from conception to losing their country. We learned that the people failed to trust the Lord for their needs and committed idol worship. They also complained to Moses, that he was leading them to their death. and they did not acknowledge God as their leader. However, Moses always pleaded with God to forgive them and He did. God would then continue to supply their needs.

Because of their continuous sins, we saw that God would send other nations to conquer them and place them into servitude until they began to cry to Him for help. At those times God would raise someone to lead them back to Him and defeat their captors. After about 400 years, of not being satisfied with the work of the Judges that God raised to help them, they requested that they have a king like the other nations had. God warned them that a king would take everything away from them. God wanted to be their King. The people did not listen and He gave them Saul. Saul started correctly but after some time His pride kicked in and God had to replace Saul with David. Some of the kings were God-fearing but many were not. Solomon, David's Son, started out walking with the Lord but then turned away. Because of Solomon's sin God split the Israeli nation into two separate countries.

10 of the tribes became Israel and 2 became the nation of Judah. Israel never had a king who walked in the ways of the Lord. Because of that God brought an end to the country of Israel and the people were scattered, never to return. Judah became the nation God used to bring us Jesus some hundreds of years later.

In the latter years of Judah's reign, God raised several prophets to warn the people of their sins. The people did not listen. Many of those prophets were jailed or killed. God finally lifted His hand from Judah for 400 years prior to the birth of Jesus. The religious leaders did not accept who Jesus was and eventually had Him crucified. Those leaders did not realize that His crucifixion was the main reason Jesus came. He took the penalty for everyone's sins. He shed His blood so that all who called upon His name would be saved. Because of Israel's sins, in 70AD God allowed the Romans to destroy Jerusalem and the Temple. Many Israelites were killed and the rest were scattered around the world for the next 2000 years.

Today, in America, we see the government writing laws opposed to what the Bible teaches. Our first mistake is that we stopped looking to God for our needs. We no longer trusted Him or His promises. We stopped making Him number one in our lives. Then we took Him and the Bible out of our schools and government buildings under the guise of the separation of church and state. Next, we made abortion legal. In 2015 the Supreme Court made homosexual marriage legal. All these laws God has condemned in the Bible. If God did not allow his chosen

Nation to get away with these sins, what makes you think that He will not punish us also?

What can we do? We must repent and return to our God and Savior. We must make ourselves heard in Washington and in our state governments with our vote. But first we must make sure we are right with God and are born again. So how do we do that? To explain this I want to start with the creation of man and how we are affected by Adam and Eve's sin.

On the sixth day of creation, God said,

Genesis 1:26 *And God said, Let us make man in our image, after our likeness: and let them have dominion over the fish of the sea, and over the fowl of the air, and over the cattle, and over all the earth, and over every creeping thing that creepeth upon the earth.*

God created us as a triune being with body, soul, and spirit. Adam had no sin which enabled him to walk and talk to God in the Garden of Eden. Genesis 2:16,17 God tells Adam that he can eat from every tree except from the tree of knowledge of good and evil.

Genesis 2:16 *But of the tree of the knowledge of good and evil, thou shalt not eat of it: for in the day that thou eatest thereof thou shalt surely die.*

God then created Eve from one of Adam's ribs as it was not good for man to live alone. As soon as Eve was created Satan stepped in and beguiled her to eat from the Tree of Knowledge of good and evil which God had forbidden. She then offered it to Adam and he ate it. Immediately they knew they were naked and made themselves a covering of leaves. Because they disobeyed God, He ejected them from the garden to fend for themselves. They were separated from God. This is spiritual death. Adam no longer had his glorified spiritual body, but in its place was an earthly body.

The Bible tells us that we will have an earthly death. We are born with an earthly body that will die.

Genesis 3:19 *In the sweat of thy face shalt thou eat bread, till thou return unto the ground; for out of it wast thou taken: for dust thou art, and unto dust shalt thou return.*

However, because God loves us so much, he made a way for us to once again obtain a new spiritual body that will live forever.

Why are we not born with a spiritual body today? One word, SIN. We are no longer born in the image of God. While we are still a triune being we are now born in the image of Adam. We are born with a sinful nature. Sin passes down from father to child. That is why Jesus had to be born of a virgin, had Joseph been His father He would not have been sin-free.

Psalms 51:5 *Behold, I was brought forth in iniquity, And in sin, my mother conceived me."*

Many believe that a child is born free of sin. The Bible tells us differently. Have you not noticed that you do not have to teach a child to be bad, but you do have to teach them to be good?

So, there you have it, we are all sinners from birth and need redemption.

Romans 3:2 *"For all have sinned and come short of the glory of God".* And what is the penalty for sin?

Romans 6:23 *For the wages of sin is death:*

It makes no difference if you think you are a good person or not. Adam's sin condemned us all. You cannot try to do good and outweigh your sins. Nor can you do penance for them.

Isaiah 64.6 *But we are all as an unclean thing, and all our righteousnesses are as filthy rags; and we all do fade as a leaf; and our iniquities, like the wind, have taken us away.*

God sees anything we try to do as filthy rags. When God created man, He knew what was going to happen, so from the beginning, He had a plan so man could be redeemed. Take notice of what God did for Adam and Eve.

Genesis 3:21 *And God made garments of animal skins for them.*

Some animal had to shed its blood for those skins. We see in the Bible why we need someone to shed His blood for us.

Hebrews 9:22 *And almost all things are by the law purged with blood; and without shedding of blood is no remission.*

In the Old Testament days, the Hebrews had to sacrifice animals so the blood would cover their sin. Those animals had to be perfect. They could have no blemish. They had to do this over and over because that blood could not take away the penalty for sin, the blood just covered it for a while. However, what Jesus did on the cross was the complete and final sacrifice. He was the perfect sin free man. We no longer must sacrifice animals for a temporary covering of our sins. Jesus made it permanent for all time.

To wash away our sins it takes a perfect man to shed His blood to pay the penalty for those sins. Where would that person come from? Because we were all born into sin, where would God find a perfect man? There was only one answer, because He loved us so much, He would send His own Son, in the form of a man, to take upon Himself the penalty for our sin.

1 Peter 2:24 *Who his own self bare our sins in his own body on the tree, that we, being dead to sins, should live unto righteousness: by whose stripes ye were healed.*

This does not mean that Jesus became a sinner, what it means is, that He paid the penalty for all our sins. We will no longer face the second death, separation from God.

You must remember that you do not go to Hell because of your sins. Jesus paid the penalty for those, the ones we committed yesterday, the ones we committed today, and the ones we will commit the rest of our lives. You will only see Hell for not accepting the gift Jesus gave us by shedding His blood on the cross. Because God's love for us is so strong, in His mercy and grace, He gave us a gift. Eternal life with Him for eternity.

How, then, do I get this gift?

Romans 10:13 *For whosoever shall call upon the name of the Lord shall be saved.*

Ephesians 2:8 *For by grace are ye saved through faith; and that not of yourselves: it is the gift of God:*

I cannot stress this enough, it makes no difference how good you are, whether you go to church every day, study your bible, or pray. Nothing you do can help, you cannot earn a gift, that is why God's love is so in-explainable, it is beyond our understanding. You must admit you are a sinner and deserve eternal punishment. You need to accept that Jesus has paid the penalty for all your sins and accept

Jesus as your Lord and Savior. Just saying this to God will do no good if it is just words. He will investigate your heart to see if you are being honest.

What happens when you do this?

2 Corinthians 5:17 *Therefore if any man be in Christ, he is a new creature: old things are passed away; behold, all things are become new.*

You will still retain your earthly body, but your spirit will be new and without sin. While we live our lives here on earth our worldly body and our Spiritual body will be in constant war. The worldly body will attempt to draw you into sin. Your defense will be trusting in Jesus and His word. That is why you need to be in the Bible studying every day.

I do not know if you will experience the same feelings I had when I accepted Jesus as my Savior, but I immediately felt as if a gigantic weight had been lifted off my shoulders. My entire life changed. My thoughts, speech, and actions completely changed. I will never forget that moment. I will never be able to thank Jesus enough for what He did for me.

God put the need, in my heart, to write this book. I had to wait constantly for Him to put in my mind what He wanted me to write. Sometimes I had to wait for weeks, then suddenly there it would be. I believe God wants America to read this book. He wants to draw us back to walking in His will. Thanks for reading and God Bless.

www.ingramcontent.com/pod-product-compliance
Lightning Source LLC
Chambersburg PA
CBHW021637120626
46545CB00002B/580